ITALY
The Best Places to See by Rail

An Alternative to the Escorted Tour

BOB KAUFMAN

The Gelato Press
916 Pleasant Street
Norwood, MA 02062 USA

ITALY   The Best Places to See by Rail
An Alternative to the Escorted Tour

Information included in this book is believed to be correct at time of publication. However, the reader should be cautioned to verify all routes and rates stated by the author with known websites on the internet. Train times stated and travel times are approximate. Hotel and attraction rates are approximate. Please consult their websites for current information. The bank exchange rate of the Euro vs. the US dollar used in this book is approximately $1.23 to purchase one Euro.

Cover photo of a "Frecciargento" ETR high speed train; bound for Rome from Venice, as it makes its way through the beautiful Italian countryside. Photo owned by Ferrovie dello Stato Italiane S.p.A. Used by permission.

Back cover photo of an ETR high speed train with Bob Kaufman and Lenore Brownstein in September, 2017 at Milano *Centrale*, courtesy of the author.

The author can be reached at
thegelatopress@gmail.com
-or-
Bob Kaufman
The Gelato Press
916 Pleasant St #9
Norwood, MA, 02062 USA

ISBN-13: 978-1985276802
ISBN-10: 1985276801

Acknowledgements:

Lenore Brownstein, for being sequestered with me for four months while I wrote this book; Ella Kaufman for choosing the sub-title "*The Best Places to See by Rail*"; Don Baine for his digital enhancement expertise; Don French for his many inputs; Sue Magod for her expert editing; Suzzette Freedlander of the DSPOT for her cover design and book layout; Henry and Jill Warner for their comments on making this book an ebook (it's coming); Scott Kaufman for his comment on the Amalfi Drive as compared to the Pacific Coast Highway; Justin Kaufman for always correcting me on the proper pronunciation of "Italy"; Franco Graceffa of La Dolce Vita Restaurant in Boston (and his cousin) for their briefing on what to do and see in Sicily; Ted Novakowski, Suzanne Slavitter, The Bensons and Robin Kasuboski for their comments about the book; Debbi Sewell for her comments; Susan Hook for her quote of "*Time and money are best spent making memories*"; Robert Fyer and Sushrut Upadhyaya of Comp Tiya for their expertise in MS Word; Trenitalia for their permission to use that beautiful cover picture of the Frecciargento; and Chris Tutolo of Raileurope for interfacing with Trenitalia in Rome.

Reviews on back cover

DEDICATION

"Happiness is finding the right travelling companion. It doesn't matter where you are going—it's who you have beside you."
Anonymous

This book is dedicated to my travelling companion and my Love, Lenore Brownstein who I met in a sand box in December of 1949.

MEET THE AUTHOR

Bob Kaufman has a passion for travel in Italy and Spain. He wrote his first book in 1983 about telecommunications. Although discontinued, it's still available on Amazon. He thought he would write his second book on Italy since few know there is an alternative to the expensive escorted tour. Bob has lots of experience on this subject. He ran those expensive tours! He is the past President of National Travel Vacations, Inc. (NTV) and for over 30 years specialized in group only tours on contract to travel agents in the USA.

Bob's an Eagle Scout, and when he is not digging clams in the summer on Cape Cod, he is enjoying the beautiful American Southwest in the winter with his travelling companion and partner Lenore. Bob and Lenore love Italian food and of course gelato.

TABLE OF CONTENTS

ITALY and SICILY

ITINERARIES A,B,C,D & E

INTRODUCTION

This book is written for seniors and the younger generation who do not wish to take an escorted tour, although you will find it a resource for any age. The font used is fourteen point Garamond, so it is larger and easier to read. The size and weight of this book makes it easy to keep in your carry-on or day-bag. I include lots of tips that only a senior would usually want to know. Like, where are the toilets and how far is the walk from the station to the hotel? Or, should I take a taxi from the station? Also, how many steps are there and where are the elevators or escalators?

I'm a senior and for almost 30 years operated group-only tours on contract to travel agents throughout the USA. Our one week escorted tours of Italy usually ran about $2500, in addition to airfare. I always wondered—If you don't take an escorted tour, how do you see Italy? If you have ever driven the Italian high speed highways known as the *Autostrada's* you know that many Italian drivers are basically maniacs. If you don't want to drive and you don't want to spend an awful lot of money, so what's the answer to spending a week or two in what I believe to be the best country to visit in Western Europe? My best advice is the subject of this book—a rail tour. And no, it's not a clickity-clackity slow train with no air-conditioning or toilets, hard wood seats and old newspapers blowing down the aisle! Things have changed dramatically over the last twenty years and more so in the last ten! So (if I have your attention) to learn more about this interesting alternative,—read on!

If you share the passion of travel like I do, and don't want to spend a lot of money to do it, then this book is for you. Sure, anyone can go on an escorted tour with hotels, meals and admissions included for one week in Italy for $2500-$5000 per person (excluding airfare). But try doing it for about $1500-$2000. I call it being resourceful. And, I don't mean staying at a one or two star hotel and eating pizza for lunch and dinner at a stand-up bar. Gone are those days from the 50's when you could travel through Italy for $5-$10 per day.

Italy's trains today are completely different than 50 years ago. In addition to amenities like those found on the airlines, high speed "TGV" type trains (pioneered in France and Japan) link the major cities of Rome, Florence, Venice, Milan, and Naples in anywhere from

60 minutes to two hours. Seats in second class are modern, reclining and comfortable. Most are equipped with power receptacles, overhead reading lights, A/C and USB outlets, luggage racks, overhead compartments and drop down tables for enjoying your favorite snack or doing work on your laptop.

All first and second class coaches are also equipped with extremely modern toilet facilities, just like those found on modern-day jet aircraft. And if you are hungry, there is always the café car for a coffee or a cappuccino and one of those Italian pastries. Or better, have it delivered by one of the coach attendants who ply the aisles with hot and cold drinks and goodies to keep you nourished. And get this—for usually about 20% more, you can go first class. What a deal!

I have broken *"Italy—The Best Places to See by Rail"* into suggested itineraries based on how much time you have available to travel through Italy on your vacation. You will find maps in the Appendix which outline exactly how many days you will need in a tight, relaxed or comfortable time frame. You need not do all of the itineraries on your first trip to Italy, and you may elect at any time to fly home after you complete one or more of the itineraries. There are five of them:

A- The Three Capitals — Rome, Florence, Venice. Fly into Rome with rail to Florence and Venice. I include optional day trips from Florence to Siena, Pisa, Lucca, San Gimignano and the Cinque Terre. The tour concludes with a flight home from Venice or you may continue with your rail journey to Milan and the Lake District.

B- Milan and the Lakes District—including Lake Como, Lake Maggorie, and Lake Lugano. This itinerary is a continuation from Venice. You can either fly home from Milan or continue over-the-Alps on the *Bernina Express*. You can also start your entire rail journey of Italy with a fly-in to Milan.

C- The *Bernina Express*, where we continue from Milan with an over-the-Alps excursion on the *Bernina Express* to Switzerland, flying home from Zurich.

D- I offer the Amalfi Extension for those of us who want to see a part of southern Italy, including Naples, Pompeii, Sorrento, Positano, Praiano, Ravello the Amalfi Drive, and the island of Capri. This concludes with a flight home from either Naples or Rome. It's best to do this in conjunction with the Three Capitals tour (A). You can start your rail tour of Italy in Naples then go north to Rome, Florence and Venice.

E- The Sicily Extensions are for those of us who are really into history (I mean ancient history). However, all will enjoy this. I include Palermo, Taormina, Trapani, Erice, Syracuse, Mount Etna; the ancient temples of Segesta, Selinunte, and the Valley of the Temples at Agrigento on the southern coast.

After spending a month in Sicily, I can tell you, this is a hidden gem of Italy and, in fact, all of the western world. I call Sicily a "sleeper".

Just a note before we get started. This book is about how to get around Italy as a tourist by rail and see the major sights. While there are hundreds of sights, I try to cover the top sights for first and second time travelers to Italy. So, don't look to this book for details on how to travel by rail from Rome to Puglia to visit your great aunt. Also, it is not a detailed book on the description and history of the sights mentioned. My suggestion is to use this book to layout your itinerary in conjunction with an in-depth travel book on Italy.

Detailed travel books provide more information than found in this book. My objective of this book is to show you how you can get from point A to point B with ease, and to structure your itinerary taking into consideration train departure times, hotel locations and walking distances, etc. I try to describe the sights which you should consider visiting, and the best way to get there, via Italy's superb and modern rail system. So best to take this book and your guide book in your carry-on, and refer to it before and during your trip.

This book will also appeal to the younger folks, ages 18-30. Many rental car agencies will not rent to the below 25 group. And, when you get to become a senior, you really don't want to drive with those crazy Italian drivers. A true vacation should be stress free and not cost a lot of money!

A rail tour meets these two objectives. And remember one thing—"Time and money are best spent in making memories!"

NO LANGUAGE PROBLEM

There is absolutely no language problem in Italy today. You are not taking a vacation to Burundi where you have got to know a little Swahili to get around. You are going to Italy.

In Italy, the equivalent of my generation and my kid's generation all speak a little English and many speak fluent English in addition to one or two other European languages. This is not the case here in America, where the majority of the Americans only speak one language. Our kids graduating high school don't usually speak English and Italian or English and Russian; some however are able to speak a little Spanish and English. You will find that this is the case in Italy. Many people will speak fluent English in addition to Italian as their primary language. However, in my opinion most of the population will speak enough English to be able to be understood and further to be able to help you.

I just love trying to converse with Italians; and I don't mean the train conductor inspecting tickets or the young lady behind the front desk at the hotel who usually will speak English. After I try to fumble some words like "where are the toilets," i.e. *doh-VEH eel twoy-let,* they usually come back in English "Oh the toilets are the second door on the right." I usually reply "Your English is far better than my Italian." They usually chuckle.

Because Italy caters to tourists, you will find that most menus in restaurants and cafes are also in English or

German or Russian in addition to Italian. All you need do is ask for the correct language menu. If you are in a restaurant which does not offer alternate language menus, then you will be mixing in with the locals and rest assured you will not be in a tourist place. In fact, they may not even have menus. The waiter will just point to a chalk black-board where the menu for the day is written in Italian, of course. I love these places!

If you find it necessary to have a language security blanket in Italy, I suggest picking up a small English to Italian phrase book, which is not a true dictionary. It is small, weighs a couple of ounces and will fit in your back pocket or your handbag. It will also tell you that *Miale Scaloppini* is Pork Scaloppini and not Veal Scaloppini. Also, it will tell you that to ask for the check, all you need say, very politely of course, is *poor favor aye, ill conto* (please, the bill). And do use the word *Grazie* as much as you can and they will always respond with *"Prego."* It does not mean pasta sauce. But it does mean "Don't mention it" or "Not a problem." In a week or two in Italy, you probably will forget that you even took that phase book with you.

The Italians absolutely love that you are trying to speak their language. They will also try to help you out with pronunciation. But watch out for different dialects, especially in Sicily. And one final point. They will always try to talk with their hands. Enjoy the warm people and their beautiful language.

Throughout this book I will refer to place names and other names in either Italian or English. So it is best to get use to this before arriving in *Italia.*

Italian	English
Ascensore	Elevator
Bagaglio	Baggage
Biglietti	Tickets
Binario (bin)	Track
Cambio	Exchange
Carozza	Coach
Centrale	Central
Centro Storico	Historic area
Colosseum	Coliseum
Ferrovia	Railroad
Firenze	Florence
Frecci	ETR fast train
Funivia	Funicular
Grande	Grand or large
Italia	Italy
Lombardia	Lombardy

Milano	Milan
Partenze	Departure
Piazza	Plaza
Roma	Rome
San Marco	St. Mark's
Scala-obili	Escalator
Sedia	Seat
Sicilia	Sicily
Siracusa	Syracuse
Stazione	Station
The Metro	The Subway
Vaporetto	Waterbus
Venezia	Venice

So now, let's get started!

CHAPTER 1

ITALY, ITALY, AND ITALY— WHAT'S SO SPECIAL ABOUT ITALY?

In 2016, almost 50 million people visited Italy. It is presently one of the top four countries in the world visited. It is usually on everyone's bucket list. Why? The three big reasons:

THE HISTORY

Italy is Civilization. Or at least western civilization, the way we know it. No other country in the world, especially the western world, spans almost 6000 years of history from pre-Roman times to the present day. It is truly the birthplace of western civilization.

The ancient Romans dating to 753 BC who inhabited the land known now as Italy gave us the foundation for most of our western languages. The Romans controlled the western world from the Middle East to the British Isles for nearly 600 years. They provided us with the basics of government still in use today. When the Roman Empire fell in AD 470, Western Europe went into decay until the Renaissance—the rebirth of the arts and the sciences. And where did it all start? You guessed it—Italy or the Italian City States as they were known then.

Italy is one big living museum of our western civilization. Everywhere you go; it is history, whether you are walking the ruins of Pompeii, the Colosseum or admiring how Michelangelo painted the ceiling of the Sistine Chapel lying on his back for four years.

What a thrill it is for first timers to visit Italy and walk the Roman Forum in the footsteps of Julius Caesar or sit on one of those stone blocks in the Colosseum.

THE PEOPLE AND THE CULTURE

I don't know of a warmer people than the Italians. Let me give you an example of what I mean. On my first trip to Italy in 1975, I boarded a city bus in front of my hotel which I thought was headed toward the Vatican. After about ten minutes on the bus, I noticed we did not cross the Tiber River. So I went over to the bus driver when he made the next stop and asked him "when do we cross the Tiber River?" He motioned that the Tiber River was the other way and suggested I get off at the next stop and catch a bus going in the opposite direction.

I exited the bus and I immediately pulled out my map of Rome to see where I was. Within three minutes, there were no less than five people trying to help me, all trying to understand my English while I tried to understand their Italian.

Italy is a place where practically everyone smiles. If they don't smile they're either having a bad day or it's just their personality. When you meet friends, you don't shake hands. Instead, you exchange kisses on the cheek. You always use salutations when greeting people. It's always *grazie* and a reply of *prego* (don't mention it). It's *arrivederci* or *ciao* or better if you really know the person —*ciao, ciao*! Greetings are expected any time of the day, especially in the evening when it's *buona serra* or sometimes just *serra*. Even those little old ladies in black dresses with little gold teeth, always seem to smile! I have always felt that the best word to describe these people is that they are indeed gracious.

THE FOOD

And let's not forget the great Italian cuisine. Italian food is best described as a cuisine which dominates the country and the regional specialties which make it even better. Northern Italian is my favorite. People ask me all the time what's the difference between Northern Italian and Southern Italian food. Simple, I say. If it's got a lot of red tomato sauce i.e. pasta of all types, lasagna, eggplant parmesan, etc., I call it Southern Italian, sometimes even Neapolitan (after Naples). If its got sauces of olive oil, butter, wine, etc., it's usually called Northern Italian. However, there is a mix of many Northern and Southern Italian dishes. No question about this— you can be enjoying veal scaloppini in Florence with a side dish of fettuccini with tomato sauce.

There are two important points which should be included when talking about the cuisine of Italy. First, Marco Polo the world explorer from Venice, in the year AD 1292 supposedly brought back pasta to Italy on his return trip from China. So, if you believe the Marco Polo story, pasta is not Italian, if you consider its history. Second, meatballs and spaghetti is American and not Italian. So you will usually never find it on any menu in Italy; best to order it in your neighborhood Italian restaurant. And one more item, let's not forget about Italian wines which I rank as an equal to French wines. That's enough for the food, I'm getting hungry.

THE ITALIAN COUNTRYSIDE

The cover of this book is typical of the beautiful Italian countryside. It is extremely diverse. You won't find a landscape like the American southwest or the Grand Canyon in Italy. What you will find is magnificent country-side with rolling hills dotted with small villages always recognizable by that gothic or medieval church. Many hilltops contain old medieval castles or even small towns, and if you don't see castles you will see ancient Roman ruins and aqueducts. The Tuscan and Umbrian provinces to the north of Rome (province of Lazio) grow grapes, olives and wheat in their fertile valleys. Closer to the central part of the "spine" of Italy are the Apennine Mountains which seem to be always in view, some of the time covered by snow.

CHAPTER 2

FOUR WAYS TO VISIT ITALY

There are four ways to visit Italy: 1) The escorted tour; 2) the FIT or commonly known as Foreign Independent Travel; 3) a private car with driver and; 4) a rail tour. It breaks down to the time you have available and the adventure pleasure i.e. enjoyment you wish to have. Couple this with how much money you wish to spend and you will have the perfect Italian holiday vacation as they say. Forget about inland waterways tours of Italy as a first time trip. There is only one that I know. *The La Bella Vita* cruises only from Venice through the fertile farmland of Northern Italy's Po River Valley. Many Mediterranean cruises stop at major Italian ports. However, "see and do" is usually limited to a few hours of a shore excursion. Hardly enough time to get the true flavor of the country.

The first way to see Italy, and what I believe to be the easiest i.e. with no hassles, is the escorted tour. I recommend this kind of tour if you care not to do it FIT or a rail tour, which this book is all about.

16

However, you will see below that the rail tour offers you more in terms of flexibility and leisure in addition to dramatic savings over an escorted bus tour. Let's look at the escorted tour.

ESCORTED TOURS

Many years ago Greyhound Bus lines, had the slogan "relax and leave the driving to us." This is so true with escorted tours. They usually include all hotels and breakfasts for each day on the tour in addition to the services of a state certified tour guide. Many times they also include what they call porterage. So all you need do is just go to your room and your bags are usually delivered within an hour. This gives you some time to take a snooze or a power nap or perhaps have a drink at the lobby bar.

One additional benefit of an escorted tour is that many operators provide transfers which allow you to reach your first hotel on the tour without a $200 taxi ride! There is usually a meet and greet person at the airport after you clear customs and immigration, holding a sign with your name. They arrange for your transport with your bags to your hotel. No need to lug them.

Once the tour starts you will be using Italian coaches (we don't call them buses). They all have toilets on board. However there are rest stops on the major roads which are known as *Autostradas* with plenty of clean facilities, snack bars and souvenirs every ten miles. Most coaches stop every hour or two for a break. Smoking is not allowed on touring coaches. Unlike the United States, Italy is certainly geared up for tourism.

Since I owned and operated a fully escorted tour company for almost thirty years, I can tell you that they are highly regimented. We always had a saying with my group tour company National Travel Vacations: "What is 6, 7, and 8?" No, it wasn't a question from the CBS TV show "Jeopardy"! What it means is 6 AM wake-up call, 7 AM breakfast and 8 AM the coach departs. The entire day is touring on an exact itinerary (knowing hour by hour where you would be) with lots of history narration. Stops are made for lunch and snacks (sometimes included). Either we go to dinner before checking into our hotel or we check into our hotel and then go to dinner at 7 PM. It is a rigorous long day.

Depending on the tour, there is some free time i.e. shopping at the Nuovo Mercato in Florence, for example, or sometimes even a free whole day on your own. In addition, tour operators obtain group tickets for museums, and other attractions, thus eliminating the need for a group to stand in line, perhaps at the Colosseum in Rome or the Academy in Florence.

In summary, the tour is highly regimented. However, on the plus side you have to do nothing except enjoy yourself. These tours are best enjoyed by seniors who don't want any hassle or anything strenuous, either mentally or physically.

FOREIGN INDEPENDENT TRAVEL

The second way of seeing Italy is known as Foreign Independent Travel or FIT. This is where you book your own hotels, rent a car, and do all those other good things i.e. get your Vatican Museum tickets online, etc. However, renting a car and driving in Italy creates high levels of stress. I don't even drive in Rome. Many of the in-town hotels in Rome, Florence and Milan do not even have garages for your overnight parking. And, if they do, you should expect to pay 25-50 Euros per night to stash your chariot.

FIT eliminates the regimentation of an escorted tour; however, you still have to do all the driving around the country, assuming you can rent a car. Many rental companies will not rent to visitors below the age of 25 or above 80.

Driving in Italy is rather "tough". I call it white knuckle driving. First the Italian drivers are crazy. Secondly, you have got to know the rules like what does "ZTL" mean when you are navigating the historic district of Rome or Florence. Combine this with limited parking, international driving signs, and trust me, you will not want to drive in Italy or you will need a Valium at the end of each day, not to mention the traffic tickets you will receive when you get home.

It's a lot of work but can be a lot of fun as you plan the entire itinerary. The internet has really made this simple and fun. You plan the day to day places you want to be and the sights you want to visit. You then decide on the hotels. It also allows you to visit and stay in small towns which may not even have a rail station (*stazione*). You need to do this if you are visiting Italy FIT or you are taking a rail tour.

Booking directories or booking engines such as *Orbitz.com, Booking.com, Hotels.com* and many more allow you to book your hotel rooms online, either prepaying them (usually with a penalty for cancellation) or booking with a free cancellation at a slightly higher rate. You can also book directly with the hotel by locating their official website and sending them an email. I provide you with lodging establishments which are only a short walk from the train station. Booking hotels now is easier than ten year ago because the internet tells you so much about each hotel or B&B. There is even more in Chapter 11 which tells you how to select the best hotel to suit your needs. This makes planning a rail tour real easy.

PRIVATE CAR WITH DRIVER

The third alternative, if you have the financial means to do, is the private car with driver. You can scour the internet for these types of services and work directly with either the car agency in Italy or a travel agent in the USA who will take care of everything. You can figure about $1000- $1500 per day per person for five star hotels, driver, car, meals, gratuities and incidentals.

A RAIL TOUR THROUGH ITALY

The fourth alternative and the subject of this book are the benefits and enjoyment of a rail tour through Italy. This book explains how to plan your Italy rail vacation with ease. But first let's look at the Italian rail system compared to the rail system in the USA.

Unlike the American rail system the Italian railway infrastructure was built and is owned by the federal government. This gives the Italian railway companies, both private and state owned, complete control over the operation of their trains. This is quite a difference between the USA, where with the exception of the Northeast Corridor (NEC), Amtrak uses private railroad tracks owned by the large freight railroads and not the government i.e. CSX, Union Pacific etc., to operate their trains.

Even though Amtrak trains are given a priority over freight trains, they usually, with the exception of the NEC, run dramatically several hours late. Delays of several hours to a full day late are rampant. On the other hand, Italian passenger trains run right on the clock. If you are running late for a train and arrive about one minute after the published departure time (*partenze*), you will find the train has departed. It is rare that trains ever run more than five minutes behind schedule. Don't compare taking a slow and delayed Amtrak train across America with taking a rail trip through Italy. They are totally different. Look at the cover of this book. That sleek *Frecciargento* ETR train will make the run from Rome to Florence in 90 minutes, averaging about 190 mph, and it won't be delayed. Even Amtrak's Acela high speed trains operating on the NEC sometimes run behind schedule 30 minutes or more.

In summary, there is absolutely no comparison between Amtrak and the trains of Italy. They are a world apart.

The state owned railway company which operates Trenitalia and Trenord is known as *Ferrovie dello Stato Italiane* or just plain FS. The tracks and stations are still owned by the government of Italy and not any railroad. Unlike the United States, the government of Italy allows private operators to use its tracks and stations. This allows the use of competing railway companies to use the physical tracks. What it means for you is that you now have a choice of which railway company to choose for travel between several of the major cities.

Taking what I call a rail tour, is simple, easy, enjoyable, and a lot of fun. However, many people don't know it exists or even know how to do it. If they are interested in seeing Italy, the first thing that comes to mind is an escorted tour. However, unlike the other ways described above, a rail tour offers the benefits of no regimentation coupled with a dramatically lower cost for the vacation, and little or no stress.

It certainly is a cost-effective alternative to the escorted tour, with many additional benefits.

Here is a quick summary of the four types of vacations by regimentation, cost and stress level:

VACATION	REGI	COST/DAY	STRESS
Escorted Bus Tour (1)	High	$300-500	None
FIT w/Rental Car (2)	None	$200	High
Private Car w/driver (3)	None	$1000-1500 (4)	None
Rail Tour	None	$150	Little

Notes:

Airfare is excluded, REGI means regimentation

Cost/Day is per person (double occupancy).

(1) Includes 4-star hotels with breakfast, lunch and some dinners, extra tours, tips, etc. Costs can be much higher with top of the line tour operators who may include all meals, tips, etc.

(2) Includes rental car, insurance, gas, tolls, parking.

(3) Includes cost also of a single room and driver meals.

(4) This is for a couple, not per person.

All four options include admissions to museums, and other places of interest.

For those wishing to learn a little about the Italian rail system, its history and those high speed trains, I offer you a short overview.

THE ITALIAN RAIL SYSTEM

The first railway line was built in 1839 between Naples and Portici. In 1861, what was called the Kingdom of Italy embarked on a plan to build a rail network from the Alps in the north to the island of Sicily in the south. In 1939, they introduced the ETR 200 with a top speed of 103 mph. Improvements were made along the way (no pun intended) and in 2009 most of the major cities were linked by trains called TAV's (*Treno Alta Velocita*) similar to the TGV's of France. These trains operate at speeds of just under 190 mph.

There are plans in the works to extend the line south from Salerno, abutting the Sorrentine Peninsular to the island of Sicily via a planned bridge over the Straits of Messina. Presently all trains bound for Sicily are pushed onto ferries and taken across the straits. There is also local train service around the island of Sicily. Please see Chapter 9 on the Sicily rail tours.

With the exception of very local regional trains, most tourists will take the high speed TGV type trains or their equivalents (called ETR's or *Frecci's*) between the major cities of Rome, Florence, Venice, Naples, and Milan. These are ultra clean, high speed and provide all the amenities you would need to make your 1-3 hour trip absolutely delightful as you see the beautiful Italian countryside wiz by at almost 200 miles per hour. First class as well as second class accommodations are available. There will be more on all this later.

There are two types of stations commonly called *stazione*. One is a terminal where double-ended trains (locomotive on each end) originate or terminate. In this way there is no need to turn the train around. The other is a through track station with several platforms which are usually reached by underground tunnels and staircases. Don't worry; in Italy everyone calls them *stazione.*

>>>TIP<<<

When boarding the double-ended intercity high speed trains, similar to the one on the cover of this book, it is best to find a seat facing the direction of travel. If your seats are reserved, as most of them are, try to pick seats in the direction of travel. You will feel more comfortable and you will not have to twist your neck to turn around and view out of the window what you have just missed. Most people on the train will not have a problem switching seats with you.

>>>>><<<<<

CHAPTER 3

CRITICAL THINGS TO DO BEFORE WE GO

You will definitely need a passport, but no visa is required if you are staying less than 90 days. And yes, you do not need any shots from your doctor. Best to make a few copies of your passport and put them in your bags should they go astray. You can also take a picture of it and stash it in your smart-phone. It is suggested that you have at least six months validity before your passport expires, otherwise most countries will not let you enter. So if your passport expires, May 1, 2021, you cannot travel to Italy (and other countries) in April, 2021. You must get it renewed.

It's best to purchase your intercity rail tickets on *trenitalia.com*, *trenord.com* or *italotreno.it/en*. If you want, consider taking the hassle out of the booking by calling *Raileurope.com* in the USA. They provide excellent advice and will book your reservations and provide your tickets for you. However bear in mind that their prices and schedules sometimes do not include all the intercity trains and rail companies and, secondly most of the time they do add a small booking fee in addition to other fees i.e. express delivery of your tickets, etc. However their effort is certainly worth the booking fee, and it is one less thing you have to worry about.

Before I call *Raileurope*, I check on-line with *Trenitalia.com* or *Italotreno.it/en* to see what their prices are. Consider also using a knowledgeable travel agent that as an agent for the railroads can provide you with information and tickets. Most of them are well versed in intercity travel in Italy, however, they may not know too much about how you get from Florence to Manarola in the Cinque Terre. It is best to check the Trenitalia website *trenitalia.com*. Also remember that when looking for tickets you must use the Italian city name. Using Florence will return you an error statement—"no such station". You must use *Firenze,* likewise *Roma* for Rome, etc.

If you will be visiting the Vatican Museum (home of Michelangelo's Sistine Chapel), you should obtain your tickets online at *museivaticani.va/*. Please see the itinerary below. You should allow two hours minimum at the museum before exiting to St. Peter's Basilica where there is no ticket is required.

If you will be going to Florence, you will need to get your tickets online for The Academy to view the *David*, and for the second day, you will need tickets to the *Uffizi* Gallery unless you will be taking the all-day rail tour to Pisa and Lucca,   Siena or the Cinque Terre or adding extra days in Firenze. Best is an afternoon ticket for The Academy, about 3 PM or 4 PM and a morning ticket for the *Uffizi* Gallery if you are planning your second day in Firenze.   Check days when the museums are closed, in that case you will have to see both in the same day i.e. the Academy in the morning and the *Uffizi* in the afternoon.

Once you have done all of the above, you are all set.

>>>TIP<<<

Oh, if you will be visiting Milan and taking in the opera, best also to get those tickets online before leaving the States. You will find internet ticketing and reservation sites listed in the Table of Popular Official Websites in the Appendix. Make sure you are dealing with the official site and not some ticket broker who will almost double the price of the ticket.

>>>>><<<<<

>>>TIP <<<

All train times and many museum reservations are made using the twenty-four hour clock. This eliminates the confusion between **AM** and **PM**. So, it is best to get accustom to this twenty-four notation. If a train is departing at **9 PM** it will show as a **21:00** *partenze*. If a museum is open in the evening, sometimes once a month, it may show a closing of **20:00**, meaning 8 PM. It should be quite easy to adapt to thinking this way. Throughout this book, often I will display times in the twenty-four hour format in addition to the **PM** format. In this way you will become familiar with the twenty-four hour notation.

>>>>><<<<<

CHAPTER 4

FIRST LET'S GET TO ITALY

For first timers visiting Italy from the USA, my recommendation is to take the Three Capitals Tour detailed in this book—Rome, Florence and Venice. If you have extra time, consider extending the trip to Naples, the Sorrentine Peninsular, Pompeii, Capri and Amalfi. There will be more about this later. In addition, also consider the extension to Milan from Venice. In this way, you will be able to visit several of the Italian lakes and yes, all by train! And finally, if you have three more days definitely take the *Bernina Express* over the Swiss Alps and return home from Zurich, Switzerland.

THE MAJOR AMERICAN AIRLINES

So, first let's get to Italy. Most of the major American airlines fly from their hubs (New York, Chicago, Atlanta, etc.) to the major cities of Italy. There is what is known as the 330 day rule. What this means is that airlines only allow you to book within 330 days of the departure day. So, you can't book a year out. However, best is to book as soon as you can and block out your departure date and city and the return. Most of the rail itineraries discussed favor a fly-in to one city and a fly-out from your final point. So there is no need to go back to Rome. This is known as an open-jaw itinerary i.e. flying into one city and out of another.

>>>TIP<<<

I suggest you don't buy your airline tickets until you are positive of your rough out or tentative schedule, since most of the tickets carry steep penalties if you wish to change them. It's best to read this entire book since you just may decide to go over the Alps on the *Bernina Express* and fly out of Zurich or perhaps take a few days and visit the Amalfi coast or Sicily and fly out of Naples or Palermo.

>>>><<<<<

You should note that if you want to do the recommended Three Capitals Tour i.e. Rome, Florence and Venice, you need to fly into Rome and out of Venice. You can also reverse the tour, flying into Venice first. However, bear in mind that many

US airlines do not fly non-stop to Venice; you will have to connect somewhere in Europe i.e. Paris, Amsterdam, Frankfurt, etc. What you don't want to do is double back to Rome by rail then fly back to the USA. This will consume an entire day (four hours on the train and then connections to the Rome airport) and you most probably will have to overnight at an airport hotel for more money. If you have to go back to Rome, here are some alternatives:

First thing in the morning fly from Venice back to Rome. The airline Alitalia has flights usually every hour to Rome that takes about an hour. However, realize that most flights bound to the USA from Italy depart 9 AM- 2 PM from Rome's Fiumicino (FCO) airport. These same airplanes then turn around and head back to Italy from the USA, 4-11 PM, arriving in Rome first thing in the morning. If you cannot get an early enough flight back to Rome (FCO) from Venice, consider going to Rome the night before and staying at a local hotel 1-2 miles from the FCO airport. You can see the table in Chapter 11 about the hotels around the rail stations and airports. My recommendation is the four-star Golden Tulip hotel on Isola Sacra, about two miles from the FCO airport. However, the flight back to Rome and the hotel alternative for the evening will add about $200 per person on to your return back to the USA. So, best is to fly back from Venice even if you must connect in Paris, Amsterdam, Frankfurt, Zurich or whatever.

TIME OF THE YEAR AND FARES

First consider the seasons. Travelling by train does create another burden in the summer. While you may elect to use porters to carry your bags (not a lot of money), bear in mind that most rail stations and terminals are outdoors and are not air-conditioned. So if you plan your trip for the summer, you will have to deal with the scorching heat of Rome and the other cities you will visit. If you are a senior, it does take a lot out of you!

In the peak summer months (high season), June through September, fares inbound to Rome and out of Venice are at their highest. In high season, expect to pay $1200-$1500 for an economy round trip ticket.

Also, you should know the following about Rome. For the month of August many restaurants close down for several weeks because of the high heat. Romans usually run to the seacoast town of Ostia or the mountains to get away from the dreadful heat. In addition, in the hot summer months many hotels in Rome shut down their air-conditioning to save on energy from about midnight and coast till 6 AM when they turn it back on. Yikes! I have been told many times that it is not a hotel policy but a Rome ordinance. So I don't know who to believe anymore.

Winter time from November through March is considered the low season. Airfares are at their lowest and hotels are a bargain. However, many days are overcast and it is the rainy season. Sometimes, Venice actually floods and you will be forced to walk around the city on temporary boardwalks erected to carry pedestrians over the flooded streets!

Winter time is also excellent if you want to include the southern part of Italy including Naples, the Sorrentine Peninsular, the Amalfi coast and even Sicily, where the winter temperatures are quite mild. On my first trip to Sorrento, I remember they were growing tomatoes in December! Also, try to avoid the days leading up to Christmas and days after New Years, as airlines hike fares since many people want to visit friends and family over the holiday season.

The best time to visit Italy is the shoulder season. Yes, yes, yes. Best are the months of April, May, mid October and November. Many of the US airlines offer rock bottom fares of about $500-$900 (non-refundable, economy) inbound to Rome and outbound from Venice. Also, many airlines which have a frequent flyer program offer reduced mileage awards for travel in the shoulder season. Do check out the American Airlines Advantage (a trademark of American Airlines) frequent flyer program for these reduced mileage awards when they are available.

SCOTTSCHEAPFLIGHTS.COM

Now if you are flexible, here's what I do. Subscribe to a website called *scottscheapflights.com*. It's only $39 a year and worth more than gold! Did it ever occur to you that airlines sometimes make mistakes setting up fares? So, say the normal fare from New York to Rome on Alitalia for March and April is $789. Mistakes happen and the computer sets it up for $389. Scott's Cheap Flights notices this because it is so out of line with other published fares. They immediately send an email and inform you which airline has the fare and the travel dates. Repeat, all they do is notify you! You must still go to Alitalia's website and book the ticket directly.

In addition to mistake fares, there are also low ball tickler fares which usually come out when they publish the eleven month (330 days) forward schedule.

Remember, you must still book the fare yourself directly on the airline's website or use another website like Google Flights or Momondo. All these fares are usually non-refundable and most airline policies may include one bag, in addition to meal service. There may be nominal fee for a reserved seat. Else if you check-in at the counter you will be given any available seat at no charge. Despite these small, sometimes extras fees, the fare is still a bargain. So, if you have the flexibility, Scott's Cheap Flights is the answer.

What you need to do is subscribe to Scotts. You only get about 20% of the deals over the website, so you need the $39 service where you get notified immediately. You must also act immediately. So if you are seriously planning on "railing" through Italy, you must absolutely JUMP at a low ball fare and book it immediately. Yes, immediately! That's right, drop everything and do it. If you don't, those fares will probably not be available tomorrow. A fare of less than $500 round trip to Italy is a steal. Consider not even telling your friends who went last year and paid $1300 a ticket. They will hate you! But do tell them about Scotts.

On my suggested Three Capitals Tour, I recommend 10-14 days. Anything short of 10 days will be a real push. You can always add extra days unless you already purchased your return flight. Also, remember since most flights are overnight, you will need at least one full day to recover. Forget that first day when you arrive. All you will want to do is drop yourself in a bed and go to sleep! So plan your trip first with this book. Then when those rock bottom fares 8-10 months out come up on Scotts, book them immediately.

>>>TIP<<<

I would strongly suggest that you read this entire book and then make your airline reservations or wait for a Scott's email. It is extremely costly to change a reservation once it has been ticketed. Think about it. It will cost you at least $1000 (with a rock-bottom fare) for a couple to fly to Italy and perhaps only $300 more to extend it another two days. It is always better to spend a few more days than a few less.

>>>>><<<<<

RESERVATIONS & RESERVATIONS

The chapters and itineraries in this book follow a format. First, I try to provide a rough out of a day-by-day journey for each itinerary. Don't feel you have to follow it just that way. If you want to add an extra day here and there, go ahead and do it. Before you book any hotels and trains, make sure you have "fixed" your itinerary. Many low fares on the Italian trains are non-refundable, just like the airlines. The same goes with certain hotel booking engines e.g. *hotels.com*, *booking*.com, *expedia*.com, etc., which offer you a lower cost for a hotel room, in exchange for a non-refundable rate. This is another reason I always favor dealing directly with a hotel rather than using a booking engine. Also, best to have all your hotel reservations before you go. Imagine arriving in Tirano, Italy only to find out that every hotel room is gone because all the dentists of northern Italy are meeting there. You certainly do not want to sleep overnight on a park bench or at the *stazione*!

STOPS EN ROUTE

When you are enjoying a rail tour, it is sometimes difficult to do an en-route stop. What I mean by this is that if you are going from Venice to Milano and want to stop for a few hours in Verona to see the Balcony of Juliet (yes, from Romeo and Juliete), it is somewhat difficult in the sense that you must exit the train in Verona and then check your baggage at the train station, for a fee of course. Problem is that there may not be any space or lockers available. Secondly, often there are long lines to retrieve your bags which may cause you to miss your departing train to Milano later in the day. If you want to see these en-route sights i.e. Verona, Orvietto, etc., my only suggestion would be to take one of those small carry-on bags with the rollers on the bottom for the week instead of the larger week-long bags, and if needed wash your cloths in a laundromat one evening. In this way you could check the bag or take it with you as you walk the streets of Verona. Not a big deal.

CHAPTER 5

THE THREE CAPITALS
ROME, FLORENCE, VENICE

ITINERARY A

ROME-FLORENCE-VENICE
ROUGH OUT:

Day 1- We fly overnight to Rome

Day 2- Arrive at Rome's Fiumicino- Da Vinci Airport, transfer to your Rome hotel, recover and light orientation
o/n Rome (o/n=Overnight)

Day 3- Ancient Rome- the Colosseum and Forum
o/n Rome

Day 4- Vatican/Monumental Rome, shopping extra day for the Baths of Caracala and the Catacombs or shopping o/n Rome

Day 5- We take a morning train to Florence
o/n Florence (*Firenze*)

Day 6- Florence (Firenze), shopping o/n Firenze
   Extra day trip to Pisa and Lucca (Chapter 10)
   Extra day trip to Siena (Chapter 10)
   Extra day trip to San Gimignano (Chapter 10)
   Extra day trip to the Cinque Terre (Chapter 10)
Day 7- We take a morning train to Venice o/n Venice
Day 8- Venice o/n Venice
   Extra day trip to the Venice Lido
   Extra day trip for the islands of Murano
   and Burano o/n Venice
Day 9- We fly home from Venice Marco Polo Airport

A word about the rough out: First, because most flights are overnight to Rome, you will need a day to recover due to lost sleep and jetlag. The rule of thumb, is you will need at least one day for each time zone to fully recover. So if you are traveling from New York, you will need six days to fully recover since Italy is six hours ahead of New York. Looking at it another way, take the flight in hours and convert to days. So, if the flight is seven hours it will take you almost seven days to recover!

If you are doing the Three Capitals Rail Tour in reverse, consider three nights in Venice instead of two. This will allow you to recover from the loss of sleep and the jetlag.

Also, I suggest you do not attempt to visit the Vatican on arrival or even on day three. There is just too much walking and you will be bushed on entry to the Vatican Museum where you will be forced to walk about a half mile just to reach the Sistine Chapel. It's just too strenuous.

On another subject, speaking of the Vatican before flying out, you need to consider the day of the week, if you want to attend a Papal audience (usually on Wednesday) or the Sunday Papal Angelus (the blessing) given by the Holy Father in St. Peter's Square (not in the Church). It is quite an event and you need not be Catholic to attend the either.

WHICH DAY TO FLY THE POND?

You can start your itinerary any day of the week except if you are considering attending any one or two of the following: the Wednesday Papal audience and/or the Sunday Papal Angelus.

If you would like to attend the Angelus on Sunday morning in St. Peter's Square, where the Pope blesses all who attend, you must fly to Rome from the USA on a Wednesday night to get to Rome on Thursday. Also you should note that you cannot visit the Vatican Museum after the Angelus, since it is closed on Sundays with the exception of the last Sunday of the month. Best to check with *museivaticani.va/*, which is the official website of the Vatican.

If you would like to attend a Wednesday Papal audience usually at 10 AM, you need to fly out on a Monday evening to arrive in Rome on Tuesday. You can obtain tickets at *papalaudience.org/* or speak to your priest about obtaining tickets. There is no charge for the tickets. With the exception of several Sundays in the hot summer, where the audience is held in St. Peter's Square, the weekly Wednesday Papal audience is held in a special auditorium next to St. Peter's.

If you want to attend the Angelus the following Sunday after you attend the Papal audience, you will have to add a few days on to your time in Rome. I would suggest several rail trips for the day i.e. Orvieto and/or Pompeii.

Construct your itinerary of the Three Capitals Tour (or if going further) and make your arrangements to fly out of Venice. Avoid very early flights i.e. 7 AM etc., if possible, since you must check in two hours early and you must figure 30-45 minutes in a taxi or water taxi etc., to get to Marco Polo Airport in Venice.

You will have to apply the same type of thinking if you are going on to Milan and the Lakes District and flying out of Milan or over the Alps on the *Bernina Express*, where you fly out of Zurich.

Best is to block out the entire trip first, think about it, and then make your hotel and rail reservations. Note that rail reservations usually cannot be made more than 120 days in advance. However, best that you make all other reservations as soon as you can. When trying to make rail reservations before the 120 day window, websites may come back with "No trains available" or some other error message. When in doubt, you should consult Raileurope's website (*raileurope.com*) or call them directly in the USA.

DAY 1- WE FLY TO ROME (ROMA)

Enjoy your overnight flight to Rome.

If you are flying non-stop from USA gateways, you should arrive in Rome in about 7-8 hours, based on New York (JFK) time. Best to add an hour for each additional time zone, so Chicago is 8-9 hours.

Remember to drink plenty of water and get up and walk around the airplane every two hours!

Personally, I find it difficult to get even a few hours of sleep. My only suggestions are: don't drink coffee or tea with caffeine, wear your blinders (usually courtesy of the airline), travel in soft lounge wear (sweats) and perhaps take an over-the-counter sleep remedy along with a baby aspirin (consult your doctor first).

>>>TIP<<<

It is best to pack your rail and museum tickets, your hotel reservation confirmations and your itinerary in your carry-on bag just in case your checked bags go astray. Don't worry, they always find them.

>>>>><<<<<

DAY 2- ARRIVAL AT ROME AIRPORT

You will arrive at Rome's FCO (Fiumicino Airport) where it occupies most of the land of the small hamlet it is named after. However, the real name of the airport is Leonardo Da Vinci Airport. Make sure, if you make a connection somewhere in Europe you do not land in Ciampino Airport, which is the local regional airport to the south of Rome serving several of the discount European operators and other regional airlines. After passing through immigration control and having your passport inspected and stamped Valid for 90 days, **NO WORK PERMITTED**, follow signs to baggage re-claim and claim your bags.

Claim your bags and if you want to take it easy, pickup one of the courtesy "trams" or luggage carts and load your bags onto it. You can also request the services of a porter to help you with your bags. They usually work the baggage control area and sometimes can be spotted wearing their bright blue outfits. Sometimes they are available just outside the large sliding doors in the un-secured area. However, my recommendation is to obtain their assistance at the baggage carousel. Inform them that you will be going to Rome on the *Leonardo Express*. It is best to provide a tip of 5-10 Euros; if you don't have Euros, a good old US ten dollar bill will also work.

You then follow the green signs marked "Nothing to Declare" and exit the secured area through the sliding doors. If you want to obtain some Euros from the ATM, now is the time to do so, or you can wait till you get to Rome, where there are plenty of machines on every corner. Definitely avoid the money changer booths marked *cambio*. The cambios state "no commission". However, you usually get a poor exchange rate. The "no commission" only means that they will not charge you a basic fixed fee to change your American dollars to Euros. The bank-owned ATM or *Bancomats* will give you the best exchange rate when using the same bank card you use stateside. By the way, if this is your first time over to Europe, make sure you inform your bank card company e.g. Bank America, etc., that you will be making cash withdrawals in Italy (and perhaps other countries in Europe) and the dates of travel. Nothing is more frustrating than not being able to obtain Euros from a *Bancomat* machine. You will find in Chapter 13 all you need to know about money, credit cards, telephone calls and more. So much for money, it's now time for our first rail adventure.

TRANSFER TO ROME *"TERMINI"*

Now follow the signs to the *Leonardo Express*. Every 15-30 minutes (except for late night hours) a train goes directly to the main rail station in Rome known as *Termini* in about 30 minutes. Make sure you buy a ticket and validate it with the green machines or old yellow machines at the station platform. Your porter can assist you.

Board the train and place your baggage in the rack if the porter has not assisted you. Note: do not place any carry-on items containing any valuables on these racks, take them to your seat and always keep an eye on them. You should note that Italian law states that you must always have your passport in your possession. All seats on the *Leonardo Express* are first class. In addition, you will find clean toilets on board. However, it is best to take care of your needs after exiting those sliding doors at the airport a few yards from the *Bancomat* machine. If you are going to use the train toilet, remember to take your carry-on if you are traveling alone, or have your traveling companion watch it.

You will arrive in about **30** minutes at *Termini*. The *Leonardo Express* makes no stops. On arrival follow the crowd to the front of the terminal where the shops are. Do not go down any of the stairs.

>>> TIP<<<

If you haven't purchased your rail tickets from Rome to Florence and from Florence to Venice, now is the time. Usually trains in the morning sell out because of day travelers doing business in either Florence or Venice. So best is to get your tickets on arrival at Rome's *Termini* rail terminal if you did not obtain them prior to leaving the USA. Avoid the automatic machines where you insert your credit card and pay for a ticket. Most of these machines are strictly for "regional" trains which make all the stops and don't offer reserved seat assignments. Even when I have taken the regional trains, I find the machines difficult to use, even though all of them offer you instructions in English.

Make your way to the long ticket counter at the plaza entrance to *Termini* and purchase your tickets for the high speed (almost 200 mph) Trenitalia Intercity (IC) trains called *Frecciarossa* (The Red Arrow). If you happen to get booked on a *Frecciarossa*-1000 which is now the fastest train in Europe, you will be traversing the beautiful Italian countryside at almost 240 miles per hour. Don't worry which type of train you will be booked on, they are all pretty fast and it is the departure time which is most important. There is usually a Trenitalia or Italo greeter helping those on the line. Make sure you are directed to an English speaking Trenitalia or Italo agent. Trenitalia and Italo take all types of credit cards. Best is to take an early morning train 8-9 AM for Florence and one for Florence to Venice. Check your dates!

Just a note, you can also travel on one of the competing high speed trains from Italo. Their trains are called *Freccibianca* (the White Arrow) or the newer *LaFrecce*. As discussed prior, it is best to book your tickets either on line or through *raileurope.com* for Trenitalia or Italo trains within the 120 day window before your rail departure dates to ensure the best choices for departure time and price. You can also go to *Trenitalia.com* or *Italotreno.it/en.com.*

Make sure you book only the high speed intercity trains mentioned above. Fares vary along with departure times. Also note that their second class basic fares are, in my opinion better than the US Amtrak system and the comfort and conveniences are far superior.

Under no circumstances book the local or regional— slow trains. These trains will take double or even triple the amount of time. The difference in cost to take the intercity high speed trains will usually be no more than $20. I always ask for the intercity (IC) high speed reserved seat train to Florence or Venice. Don't worry they fully understand. Also, remember that all seats are reserved. The ticket agents will ask you how many people are travelling and will always try to give you adjoining seats or seats facing each other.

Here is the approximate running times and costs between the two cities:

Rome *Termini* Station – *Firenze* SMN (Santa Maria Novella) 90 minutes. Basic economy (non-refundable) second class ticket cost $25-40.

Florence SMN (Santa Maria Novella) to Venice Santa Lucia, 2 hours. Basic economy (non-refundable) second class ticket cost $50-60. Please remember that these costs are approximate and vary by time of day, class of service, refundable vs. Non-refundable and by how far in advance you purchase the tickets.

The times will become shorter once the ETR-1000's are certified for running at 240 miles per hour. Consider going first class for a few dollars more, if available. You get a wider seat, more space to put you luggage and certain amenities such as coffee, a soft drink and a newspaper (yes, in Italian). These vary by route and train, just like the fares. Most of the time beverages and snacks are delivered via a rolling cart in the aisle; there is no need to walk to the café.

>>>TIP<<<

Now, if you have some time after purchasing your intercity rail tickets, your eyeballs have not yet dropped out, and feel you are up to it, stop by the cell phone store at *Termini* and purchase an inexpensive Italian cell phone with a SIM card. It will cost you about $40 and allow you to make calls within Italy and also to the USA. See Chapter 13 for additional alternatives to making telephone calls. Remember, the cell phone people will need to make a photo copy of your passport for security purposes, and usually the phone will not be active for 24 hours. Make sure your passport is returned before leaving the phone shop.

>>>><<<<<

CHECKING INTO YOUR ROME HOTEL

You are now ready to check into your nearby hotel. If you are not staying at one of the hotels close to *Termini*, you must work your way to the taxi line and take a licensed taxi to your hotel. To avoid a 200 Euro taxi fare, it's best to ask the driver before you step into the taxi about how much is the total fare to your location. Most drivers are honest, will speak a little English and will understand you.

Exit the *Termini rail* terminal and head for your hotel. If you are within walking distance and don't want to drag or roll your bag, summon a porter and ask if he can take your bags two or three blocks over to the hotel. It's best to use Google Maps to locate your hotel in relationship to *Termini*, print out the instructions (before you leave the USA) and keep it with your passport. In this way you know that all you have to do is exit to the right (via Marsala) and walk one block up to the hotel. If you try to use Google Maps (*maps.google.com*) on your American cell phone without WIFI, it will pretty much eat up all of your 250Mb monthly data allowance (if roaming with Verizon) in about 5-10 minutes!

Anyway, find your hotel; request a quiet room and then sack out for at least three hours. Just a note, in Italy and many other hotels around the world, the front desk person will take your passport from you for several hours or perhaps till the next morning. Many times they report names of all guests to the local police department. Don't worry; it's not a big deal! Just remember to ask for your passports back before you head out of the hotel. In Italy, it is a federal law that if you do not have Italian citizenship; you must be in possession of your passport while in the country. This means that when you are walking around, on a train, etc., you should have your passport with you. It's best not to pack them in your luggage bag and leave them in your hotel room.

In addition to passport protocol, many Italian and European hotels have not kept up with the newer technology utilizing electronic key cards and you will have to surrender that one pound key they give you when leaving the hotel. Don't worry about security of your room. And, by the way, avoid leaving expensive items in your room in plain view, or just don't take them with you. There is an old rule: If you can't bear to part with them, don't bring them. This goes for anywhere you travel and not just in Italy!

ROME RECOVERY

After your "recovery" nap, take a shower and freshen up. You are now ready to begin Day 2 activities. Try to avoid sleeping more than three hours, else you will sleep all day and into the night, wake-up at 3 AM and wonder where to have breakfast! The objective is to force your body to get on Italian time, best known as CET (Central European Time).

>>>TIP<<<

Make sure you set an alarm on your smart-phone to avoid oversleeping.

>>>>><<<<<

However, before going out of your hotel, best that I summarize the highlights of Rome not to be missed. You can plan the next three days accordingly based on time of day, weather, etc.

You should not feel that you must follow this rough-out, even though this is what I recommend from my numerous trips (I stopped counting after 20) to Italy.

So here are the best sights to see not necessarily in the order of importance, but grouped by historical time period and stress to your body. You will have three days in Rome before you depart for Florence. With the exception of Wednesday and Sunday, when special events happen at Vatican City, you can plan your days by the weather or by the most important sights to see.

Note also, depending on your flight arrival time into Rome Airport you will hopefully have a half day of sightseeing in Rome or more. If you arrive real early, about 7 AM, you will probably check into your hotel about 9 AM. If your room is ready—great! Otherwise, you will check your bags (or have the front desk watch them) and set-out for your Rome orientation. In any case, even with an arrival about noon, you will still have a half day for the orientation.

ROME ORIENTATION

The *Grayline* (*graylinerome.com*) and other day tour operators provide four hour orientation tours and all-day tours. Many of them will pick you up at your hotel or an adjacent hotel. You can pick up brochures in any of the hotels. However, bear in mind that hotel concierges make commissions off these tours and will request payment in cash in lieu of a credit card for booking one for you. It's best to telephone from your room (a local call) and book the tour directly with your credit card, thus avoiding any commission which may be added. You can also check this out before leaving the USA since many include the Colosseum and Forum on their orientation tour with admission tickets. So it may be best to just book a four hour orientation tour. These tours operate late into the day returning about 7 PM to your hotel or a convenient drop-off point. I would suggest a late afternoon tour with an overview of the Spanish Steps, Trevi Fountain, Piazza Navona, the Pantheon and more.

DAYS 3 AND 4 ANCIENT AND MONUMENTAL ROME, THE VATICAN, THE RENAISSANCE

I have divided the next two full days in Rome into three categories. There may be some overlap. With the exception of the Vatican, which is a separate country *The Holy See*, Rome seems to be a collection of lots of the items below. There is no rhyme or reason to their placement in the "*Centro Storico*" (historic district) and the adjoining areas of historic Rome. So be prepared to see Trajan's Market, AD 100 (the first indoor shopping mall) across the street from the Monument Vittorio Emanuele II built in 1911, on your walk over to the Colosseum, AD 80. Best is to consult a travel book on Rome or the internet for all the history on each specific sight you will be visiting.

There is lots of walking, so best to plan a morning visit to the Vatican Museum and St. Peter's. Days 3 and 4 should be planned well, with visits to the sights of ancient and monumental Rome. Likewise, visits to the Renaissance treasures should also be visited. I have prioritized them. Walking in Rome is quite easy. With the exception of a few small hills the place is all flat. The entire *Centro Storico* is no more than one square mile.

Since this book is merely an overview of Rome and the major attractions of Italy which can be reached easily by rail, I cannot emphasize enough that it is best to supplement this book with a good tour guide or travel book on Italy.

Here is just a partial list of some of the sights broken down by category:

ANCIENT AND MONUMENTAL ROME

Below I have listed about eight of the 200+ ancient monuments from the Republic of Rome in my order of importance to visit. They are:

The Colosseum and the Roman Forum,

   Closed Mondays, purchase tickets online, see Table of Popular Official Websites in the Appendix;

The Baths of Caracalla;

Circus of Maximus;

Castel St. Angelo (near the Vatican, you can't miss it, it's on the Tiber river about one half mile before St. Peter's);

The Catacombs, there are many, just pick one and observe the hours of operation as many are closed for siesta;

The Apian Way and Quo Vadis;

The Aurelian Walls;

Trajan's Market;

Trajan's Column;
The Pyramid of Rome (Yes, there is one here no need to go to Egypt).

MONUMENTS OF ROME

Note- some of these are actually Renaissance Rome monuments. Many are open late at night or just don't close:

The Pantheon- Ancient Pagan temple, etc;

The Trevi Fountain (throw the three coins over your shoulder);

The Spanish Steps (walk down them) from the Metro elevator;

The Monument to Vittorio Emanuel II (a/k/a "The Wedding cake");

The Piazza Navona;

Piazza di Popolo;

And do visit the Colosseum at night.

RENAISSANCE ROME

The Roman Renaissance took place from the mid 15th century to the middle of the 16th century. The masters include (to name a few): Michelangelo, Raphael, Donatello, and Brunelleschi all left their mark on Rome. In addition, many of the artists even painted scenes with the ruins of Rome as backdrops. After the Renaissance, the Baroque period of art and architecture commenced. The Trevi Fountain is one of the best known Baroque monuments. It is also worth a visit at night when it is dramatically lit up.

Michelangelo's magnificent sculpture the *Moses* is located only three blocks from the Colosseum and housed in the church of San Pietro in Vincoli (St. Peter in Chains). In my opinion, this is second only to the *David* in Firenze. A must to see after you exit the Colosseum and the Roman Forum.

Be sure to see Bernini's *Apollo and Daphne* which is housed in the Galleria Borghese. Also on display are many works by Titian, Ruben and Raphael. Nice thing about the Galleria Borghese is that it is located in the Borghese Gardens. The entrance is located at the beginning of the Via Veneto a few blocks from the Spanish Steps. There is a small entrance fee. Best to book online before you leave the USA at *tosc.it/biglietti.htm.*

You will find Borromini's *Prospecttiva,* located in the Palazzo Spada which is located right off the Campo de Fiori street market held every day, except Sunday. The *Prospecttiva* painting is an illusion whereby you observe a hallway flanked by columns which appears to be about 100 plus feet in depth. In reality the painting is on a single plane. Admission to the Palazzo Spada is about five Euros.

Another sight not to miss is the mosaics of the Santa Maria in Trastevere across the Tiber River where the tiles adorn the inside of the dome of this church which dates to about the fourth century. Within a five minute walk of the church are about 100 restaurants, cafes and stand-up bars, ideal for lunch or dinner.

Two additional must-sees include *The Gallery of Mirrors* which is part of the Palazzo Doria Pamphilj located only a few blocks from the Piazza Venezia on the Via del Corso. The *Gallery of Mirrors* looks like the *Hall of Mirrors* in Versaillis, France. The other is Bernini's statue *Ecstasy of Saint Theresa* which is located in the Santa Maria della Vittorio Church, just a few blocks from the Piazza Barberini and the American Embassy.

THE VATICAN AND CATHOLIC ROME

The Vatican is a self-contained country within the city of Rome. It was created by the Lateran Pacts signed in 1929, which gave it its own status of a separate country. There are no Roman or Italian police or soldiers inside the walls of the Vatican. The Vatican has its own security forces including those colorful Swiss Guards.

The Vatican also known as *The Holy See* (Holy Seal) is one of the smallest countries in the world, if not the smallest. Its population is about 600 people. It is the international home to the Catholic Church Religion and contains their offices, living quarters, a pharmacy, a radio and TV station and an underground railroad station for the Holy Father (The Pope), and its own post office. In addition, it is surrounded by a wall two miles long with high security. The Vatican has their own police department, a security force and of course those colorful Swiss Guards. Within the walls is a 109 acre beautiful campus environment.

You will need a minimum of four hours to take in the Vatican Museum and Saint Peter's Church and square. After exiting the Museum you can enjoy a lunch on many of the nearby streets. My favorites are the outside cafes on Borgo Pio. When exiting the Vatican Museum, bear to your right and follow the people waiting in line against the walls of the Vatican. It's about an 8-10 block walk. Just look for the Borgo Pio on your left about two blocks before you reach the entrance to St. Peter's Square with all those round columns. If you arrive at St. Peters square you missed it. For a such a high touristed area, it amazes me that the prices of all the eateries are on the low side. There are also some good places for lunch after you exit the Vatican Museum. Just go to your left for about 100 yards, look to your right, and you will see stairs down to a street below named Via degli Scipioni. Here within a three block radius you will find lots of places to have lunch.

The Vatican is the home of the Vatican Museum with its Sistine Chapel where its world renowned ceiling depicts scenes from *The Book of Genesis* painted by Michelangelo in the years 1508-1512. And no, he did not paint the ceiling on his back! That was only in the movie *The Agony and the Ecstasy* (1965, movie by Twentieth Century Fox, book by Irving Stone). The treasures of the Vatican Museum and the Vatican are housed in the hallways and the galleries of this mind-baffling museum. It will take you 30-45 minutes after passing through security to walk the hallways and stairs which finally lead you to the Sistine Chapel. Suggest you check out the facilities in the lobby of the museum before starting your tour. You will get another chance to use the facilities just before entering the Sistine Chapel.

An Alternative to the Escorted Tour

Here are the details you have to know about the Vatican Museum and your visit to St. Peter's. If you have not purchased your tickets for the museum before you left the United States, either arrive at 7 AM or be prepared for a 1-2 hour wait in a line almost a half mile long! Yikes! Make sure you are on the line to purchase tickets. Enjoy that large coffee and those Italian pastries. If you have your tickets already, you should be on that very short ticket holder's line.

Once inside the lobby area of the Vatican Museum, you will be required to pass through security. It is the same as the airports. You should not bring any large "rucksacks or nap sacks". Men, make sure you do not have any small "pen knives" with you. There is a good chance you will not be returning through this lobby as you will go directly into St. Peter's Basilica after viewing the ceiling of the Sistine Chapel.

Both women and men must adhere to the dress rules of the Vatican and St. Peter's church. You should consult their website which is museivaticani.va/. If you are not dressed appropriately the Swiss Guards and security will deny you access.

Be prepared for a lot of walking at the Vatican Museum. You also have to climb several flights of stairs (there are elevators if you are somewhat physically challenged). Everyone is headed for the same place so just follow the crowd.

Once inside the Sistine Chapel, there is no talking and no use of flash cameras. You really need only 5-10 minutes here to just view Michelangelo's marvel. It's quite a piece of artwork considering that it was painted about 400 years ago.

After the viewing, you will note that there is an exit door on the right and one on the left. If you take the exit from the chapel via the door on the left you will be forced to walk back the entire length of the museum to the main entrance where you entered. You will then have to walk about a half mile around the walls of the Vatican to enter St. Peter's Basilica and clear security again. However, there is an easier way.

If you want to go directly to St. Peter's Basilica you must exit the door on the right. However, there is a sign *Gruppo Solo* and an attendant who stands guard. This door is used for groups as it saves about one hour on a group tour. Just tell the guard at the door that you have been separated from your group which went out this door about five minutes ago. He will open the door and usher you out. In this way, you will not have to walk all the way back to the main entrance of the Vatican Museum, then all the way around the Vatican wall, then have to clear security again at St. Peter's. You will go down several flights of stairs and, presto, you will be at St. Peter's. Also note, just to the right of the base of the stairs are the rest rooms. So it will be a good idea to make a pit stop here before entering the largest church in the world.

If you want to spend some more time at the Vatican Museum, you will also find a cafeteria here with magnificent views of the Vatican gardens. From the Sistine Chapel, you need to go out the door on the left which will keep you in the museum instead of dropping you down into St. Peter's. Also, if it's around the lunch hour consider taking the long walk back and having lunch outside the museum before visiting St. Peter's. If you are going to the dining spots on the Borgo Pio, go out the right hand door (*Gruppo Solo*) and exit via St. Peter's Basilica as you will find this route much shorter than going back through the museum to the main entrance.

ST. PETER'S BASILICA

St. Peter's Basilica is the largest church (in terms of square footage in the building itself) in the world and one of the most famous examples of Renaissance architecture. Supposedly the church is built over the remains of Saint Peter, one of the twelve apostles of Jesus Christ. This is a must see, even if you are not Catholic or not even Christian.

You will need a minimum of a half hour here (more like an hour) to marvel at the opulence and the grandeur of this beautiful church. Stroll around the church and view the beautiful works of art and several preserved popes under glass. Yes, they are real. And finally, do view one of Michelangelo's most famous sculptures, *The Pieta* on your left as you exit the church. It's easy to find, just look for the crowd.

If you have extra time you can climb to the top of the Dome of St. Peter's. There may be a small admission charge and I believe an extra seven Euros for the elevator. You still have to climb over 300 steps after you exit the elevator. Yikes!

After you complete your visit to the Vatican and St. Peter's, about 1-2 PM and you have not had lunch; it's time to find the Borgo Pio. You can take your pick of numerous restaurants, as you walk down Borgo Pio toward the Tiber River.

Hopefully, after lunch you do not want to go back to your hotel and take a siesta, as many Romans often do. So, best is to take on Monumental Rome. I might note that many restaurants in Rome do not open till 7:30 (19:30) or 8 PM (20:00) so you will have plenty of time to get some rest before dinner.

MAKE ROME EASY

Rome is a walking city. If you plan your day, you can minimize all that walking. Seniors take note!

Best is to obtain one of those maps from the concierge of your hotel. Then circle all the sights you wish to visit. Now, all you need do is connect those circles. You can also order from *Amazon.com* the *Michelin Streetwise Rome Map.* This is a laminated fold up map. It is ideal for marking and planning your route. Do bring a few of those water based markers with you, else an eyebrow pencil will also do. Here is one of the walks I recommend:

1. You start at the top of the Spanish Steps;
2. Down the steps, go left on the Via Barbuino;

(Note this becomes "Corso")
3. Then the Trevi Fountain;
4. Then the Pantheon;
5. Then Piazza Venezia;
6. Monument to Vittorio Emanuele II;
7. Then Trajan's Market;
8. Then the Roman Forum;
9. Next the Colosseum;
10. then Michelangelo's The *Moses*.

And if you are too tired or just want to save those steps, consider Rome's subway known as the *Metropolitana di Roma*.

THE METROPOLITANA DI ROMA

If you have been to Rome as many times as I have, you know the following facts: A) You don't drive in Rome; B) You avoid taking taxis because you can sit in traffic a long time with the meter running; and C) it can cost you a lot of Euros. On one occasion, I actually told the taxi driver to just let me off here and I walked the remainder of the way.

Rome is a walking city, especially if you are making your way around the *Centro Storico*, i.e. the central historical district. However, an alternative to the taxi and those long walks e.g. from the Colosseum to the Spanish Steps, it's best to just take the *Metropolitana,* Rome's excellent subway system.

The *Metropolitana* consists of three lines which crisscross the city. They're known as Lines A, B and C. The trains are fast and will get you from *Termini* to the Spanish Steps in ten minutes and save you that long walk. You can buy tickets in the machines and it's quite simple. You must make sure you validate them by placing them in the ticket barrier i.e. the old turn-style, now with high tech ticket readers, like most other metros including New York. The ticket is good for one ride anywhere on the system.

You should forget about Line C, as only parts of it are open and it is still under construction. What's nice about the Metro is that Lines A and B intersect under the *Termini* rail terminal and changing from one line to the other is easy. In addition, with the exception of the Vatican, (which is several blocks away from the Vatican Museum) it's easy to use the Metro to reach the Colosseum, The Roman Forum, the Circus Maximus (Circo Massimo) and the area of the Spanish Steps, including a short walk to the Via Veneto.

Speaking of the Spanish Steps, I should note that if you want to go to the top of the Spanish Steps (*Spagna* Station) you will find an elevator in the station. So there is no need to climb all those steps up to the beautiful church on Via Sistina known as Trinita dei Monti. The church appears in all the photos of the Spanish Steps. Take the elevator to the top and walk down the steps to the *piazza*. Afterwards enjoy lunch at one of my favorites—*La Rampa* right under the Spanish Steps, just behind the American Express office in the corner where it is hidden.

Now if you want to reach the Vatican Museum you need to take Line A in direction of *Battistini* and get off at the *Ottaviano S. Pietro* stop which is the one after *Lepanto.*

You must be extra cautious on the Metro. Keep your hands in your pockets and ladies do clutch that zippered bag. I always suggest you stand in a corner of the car, away from everyone else. Also, do not fall for odd ball pick-pocket pranks like dropping coins on the floor so you are forced to help a person out and pick them up. If you take short rides and mind your things you will be fine. For more info, consult the Metro website at *atac.roma.it*, for a printable map.

AN EXTRA DAY IN ROME

If you have an extra day to spend in Rome consider shopping on the Via dei Condotti (at bottom of the Spanish Steps), where you will find the Gucci, Dior, Louis Vuitton and others. Afterwards, have a café at the base of the Spanish Steps or better yet, climb it and have a café on Via Sistina.

Once on the Via Sistina, it's only a few blocks to the Via Veneto where you can stroll this elegant street and gaze at the shops, restaurants and hotels where the Hollywood rich and famous hung out in the '50's. It is also home to the American Embassy to the Republic of Italy and the *Holy See* (The Vatican). All you need do is keep asking directions *Dough-Veh* (where is) Via Veneto? However, they probably will answer you in English and motion with their hands.

If you want to visit the Jewish quarter you will find it quite interesting. Here you will find the Great Synagogue of Rome which faces the Tiber River. It was built in **1901** and is now part synagogue and part museum. Of interest are the bakeries in the old Jewish section and other shops. Note the place quiets down about 4 PM (16:00) on Fridays and all day Saturday for the Sabbath. The nice thing about the

Jewish Quarter is that it's only a short walk from the Piazza Navona.

DAY 5– TRAIN TO FLORENCE

If you have not purchased your morning tickets to Florence (*Firenze*) on the high speed train the *Frecciarossa* or the *Italo Frecciabianca*, you will have to arrive at the *Termini* rail station about one hour prior to train departure and hopefully there will be seats available on this all-reserved seat train.

The train ride is only 90 minutes. However, if your plan is to have a snack or a light breakfast on the train, now is the time to grab some fresh croissants or a breakfast sandwich at the many take away cafés at *Termini*. Also, if one of your hands is free, consider a coffee or a tea. Purchasing food on the train, when available, is extremely pricey. Expect to pay 3-5 Euros for a cup of coffee and 7-10 Euros for a breakfast sandwich. So best to board the train "provisioned".

Do check out the facilities before you board the train. They are located on the lower level. So you must go down the escalator near the Marsala entrance. Have your traveling companion watch the bags, etc. Also note, most facilities now require a one Euro coin for admission. Make sure you have a pocket full of them.

Most of the time you need not validate tickets for day of travel and reserved seats since, technically, if you don't use them you lose them. So don't worry about validating. However, you still will be visited by a train conductor who will inspect your tickets, so make sure you have them available.

Trains in Europe depart on time. If the train departs at 8:30 AM and you arrive at 8:31 AM you most probably will not find the train on the track. The rule is to board the train once it is announced on the big electronic board. Find your train by track number or "*Bin*", short for *binaria.* Ask the train conductor or read the side of the car for the destination, or better ask others boarding the train. You certainly want to board the train to *Firenze* SMN and not the train to *Napoli* (Naples)! You should be on the train at least 20 minutes before departure.

Note, if you are running late, hop on the first car you come to and just get on the train. You can walk through the train from car to car until you find the correct one. Those big numbers on the car indicate first and second class i.e. "1" and "2". Some cars (depending on train and railway company) may be split, i.e. first class on one end of the coach and second class on the other end of the coach.

If you have heavy luggage, it is best to get on the train with the 20 minute rule. If you only have one of those carry on rolling bags you can walk the train easily.

Here are some tips on how to read the lighted signboards on the cars. First, if you haven't looked at your ticket before boarding, do so now. It will indicate the car number *carozza* and then the seat *sedia* numbers. Walk on the platform and find your car number and hop on the train. If your bags are heavy (see how to pack in the back of the book), it's okay to ask for help from one of those strapping young Italian men.

Then locate your *sedia* or seat number. You must walk the coach you are assigned to, 'til you spot your seat number. The numbers usually don't go in order, since there are several configuration layouts. It's not like an airline i.e. row 24, seats A,C, DEFG, HJ etc.

Once you find your seats, look at where to stow your bags. On the high speed inter-city trains (*Frecci's*) depending on the configuration, here are your choices:

On entrance to the rail car (carriage or *carozza*) you may find those handy luggage storage areas. Some cars are designed with back to back seats i.e. facing each other. This creates a nice cavity to drop your bags behind your seat. If all else fails and hopefully your bags are light, lift them gently onto the baggage rack in the front of the car or over you. Once again, if you care not to break your wrist or something else, ask one of those Italian young guys to assist you. I might note that first class usually has more places to stow your bags.

The rail line to *Firenze* is a fast 90 minutes through mostly farm country dotted with small villages. The ticket inspector will say hello to you and shortly you will arrive in *Firenze's* Santa Maria Novella (SMN) train terminal. The station is named after the church directly opposite the station.

On arrival find your hotel (you should be able to walk a few blocks to it) and check your bags if your room is not ready. If your hotel is located to the left of the station as you exit the train, you will find an exit to your left so there is no need to drag your bags through the front of the station unless your hotel is directly on a path in front.

After checking into your hotel, do enjoy lunch and a gelato as you walk over to The Academy (official name is *Galleria dell' Accademia di Firenze*) to view the *David*. If you have not purchased your tickets on the internet for a timed interval of entrance i.e. 2:30 PM (14:30), be prepared for a two hour wait on that long line. If you stay at any of the hotels on my list, it should take you no more than fifteen minutes to walk over to The Academy.

INTRODUCTION TO *FIRENZE*

First a few words about history. The Roman Empire according to historians officially started in Rome in 27 BC and ended in Rome in AD 476. There were no nations in Europe at that time. After the fall of Rome, Europe supposedly (I wasn't around so I can't tell you exactly what happened) fell into the dark ages. This period was also referred to as medieval times or the Middle Ages.

From about AD 500 to AD 1500 there was no Roman army to protect the people from marauding tribes, no construction of a vast network of roads, no aqueducts were constructed to bring water into a town, and no public buildings were erected. Rome was in fact "dead" and so was everything else which gave us the foundations of western civilization. Today, we take all this for granted—local and regional government, a financial system, money, taxation, an army and navy for defense to name a few. Now they were all gone. There were some positive things, thank goodness the evil things were gone like the Roman gladiators and Roman slaves.

Medieval times brought about the feudal system of castles, lords and all that other stuff. The king (or lord) of the area had a castle and in return for the deliverance of farm grown items, cattle, goats and other items grown outside the castle, the king offered protection to the people. If a marauding tribe threatened to make war with the local people i.e. take all the food and live stock, burn the hamlet, kill all, take the women, etc. the lord would have the locals come into the castle and help with the fight i.e. pour the boiling oil over the ramparts, help with the bow and arrows and all that stuff. Noting really happened in Europe except lots of feudal wars, plagues and minor construction of some churches. This lasted until the birth of the Italian city states i.e. Florence, Venice, Naples, etc.

Florence is the birthplace of the Renaissance or at least the Italian Renaissance. It is the capital city of the Italian region known as *Tuscany*. The historic area of *Firenze* is a UNESCO World Heritage site. And yes, it's in *"1,000 Places to See Before You Die" by Patricia Schultz,* as well as most of the places you will visit in Italy. Italy leads all countries, having 47 UNESCO World Heritage sites.

You might consider a few more days in *Firenze* if you have the time. Suggest you take a look at Chapter 10 —The Florence Day Trips. For now, here are my recommendations. The three main sights to see here which are of equal importance are Michelangelo's the *David* at The Academy, the *Uffizi* Gallery and lastly the Duomo complex. For the shopping, it's definitely the Ponte Vecchio Bridge over the Arno River, the Nuovo Mercato and the shops along the Via Por Santa Maria from the Mercato to the Ponte Vecchio.

Fortunately, you are all lucky. All of the above are just a few blocks from each other. And get this—most of the walking is via limited small streets where only taxis and pedestrians are allowed.

Most of the sights of *Firenze* relate to The Renaissance, that rebirth of the arts and sciences. Don't look for any ruins from the Roman empire of - 2000 years ago; you probably won't find them, except if you are looking at the ruins below the Duomo, which are free to visit. You will, of course, find the remains of ancient Roman aqueducts in the countryside around *Firenze.*

As a side note, *Firenze* is an excellent jumping off spot for an afternoon in Pisa or full day trips to: Pisa and Lucca, Siena, San Gimignano, and the Cinque Terre. These five towns, which are all reachable by rail, are discussed in detail in Chapter 10. I would strongly suggest that if you have the time, do add several days more to see these unique towns/sights before heading on to Venice.

MICHELANGELO'S THE *DAVID*

One of the greatest artists, sculptors, and architects of the Italian Renaissance was Michelangelo di Lodovico Buonarroti Simoni   commonly known as just Michelangelo.   His most famous works include the ceiling of the Sistine Chapel in the Vatican Museum, the *Last Judgment,* the *Moses,* the *Pieta* (just on the right as you enter St. Peter's) and the design of St. Peters, as the successor architect to   Antonio da Sangallo; Michelangelo lived from 1475 to 1564.

Of all his works, at the top of the list, is without question the *David*, which is the *"David"* from the Old Testament i.e., from the story of David and Goliath. Michelangelo's masterpiece was created 1501-1504, and chiseled out of one massive block of marble. It weighs about 13,000 pounds. And yes, it's in the book *"1,000 Places to See Before You Die."* And yes, you must see it. Make sure you purchase your tickets before leaving the USA; else you will have to wait in a long line 1-2 hours to obtain tickets. Check out the website at *academia.org/*.

THE DUOMO OF *FIRENZE*

You should have enough time and energy to take a 15 minute walk over to the Duomo of *Firenze* (Florence Cathedral). It is another massive church. However, this church is also a masterpiece of art. It was started in 1296 and finally completed 140 years later. What is most impressive about the church, its Baptistery and the *Campanile* (the tower) is the striking pink and green tiles which comprise the facade of the three buildings. It is, of course, a UNESCO World Heritage Site. There is no admission charge to enter.

In 1965-1974 excavations took place under the floor of the Duomo. Roman houses and ruins of a former cathedral were unearthed. You may view these remains anytime the church is open. Just follow the line. Once again there is no admission charge.

By now you are probably out of energy to do anything else in *Firenze*. If you haven't had that delicious gelato, do so now as you stroll back to your hotel for a snooze before dinner.

DAY 6-THE *UFFIZI* & SHOPPING

Without question, the *Uffizi* Gallery ranks among the top museums of the western world right up there with The Louvre, Prado, Rijks, Orsay, Vatican and the British Museum. If you are into the treasures of the Renaissance, this is the place. You will need to purchase your tickets before you leave the USA. No exceptions here. My first time to the *Uffizi* I saw the electronic signs outside stating "Next Available Tickets in Three Days." I was shutout. The *Uffizi* would have to wait for my next trip. So what's the *Uffizi* all about? Simple, it contains the masterpieces of the Renaissance in the form of paintings and sculptures; also, artwork dating to as late as the 18th century. It spans fifty rooms with artists most of us never heard of with the exception of several pieces by the masters i.e. Michelangelo, Boticelli, and Raffaello to name a few. The original building used to be the offices of magistrates and judges who conducted official business, thus the name *"Uffizi"* meaning "official." You will need a minimum of two hours here. And remember that many museums are closed on Mondays. Their website is *florence-museum.com/*. I should note you can also purchase the tickets to The Academy to view the *David* on the same website. Oh, one more thing. See the *Uffizi* Gallery right after breakfast since there is a lot of walking through the galleries and you will be drained by lunch time.

>>>TIP<<<

It is best to start on the second floor with all those famous paintings and work your way down. If you have any energy left, go back and start on the top floor with all the sculptures.

>>>><<<<

SHOPPING IN *FIRENZE*

Shopping in *Firenze* runs the gamut from high end gold and plenty of gold to items costing below ten Euros. My suggestion always is to have lunch first after exiting the *Uffizi* Gallery. There are two good areas for this. Next to the *Uffizi* Gallery is the Piazza delle Signoria. You can take your pick of numerous restaurants, stand-up bars and outdoor cafes. My favorite is the *Il Bargello*. I love it because all the food is like home cooking. The other location for numerous eateries is the area abutting the Piazza del Mercato Nuovo about three blocks from the Piazza delle Signoria.

After lunch, start your shopping at the Mercato Nuovo (short for the Piazza del Mercato Nuovo) and then work your way toward the Ponte Vecchio bridge by strolling down the Via Por Santa Maria. Walk over the Ponte Vecchio and enjoy looking in the windows of all those gold jewelry shops. When you reach the end, have yourself a gelato, then turn-around and walk back to your hotel for a siesta before dinner.

If you are interested in a unique restaurant directly across the river between the Ponte Vecchio and Ponta Santa Trinita bridges, I always recommend the *Osteria Cinghiale Bianco*. *Cinghiale* is Italian for wild boar; yup, the forest animal. And this place dishes it out several ways. I love the *Cinghiale* tossed in pasta. You will not be disappointed and you will find the prices quite reasonable as this is a basic "Risto" (restaurant).

Please read Chapter 10 for the rail day trips to Pisa and Lucca, Siena, San Gimignano and the Cinque Terre.

If you are continuing to Venice please read on. I might note that most of the European airlines serve *Firenze* directly from their hubs i.e. Frankfurt, Paris, Amsterdam, etc. If you cannot fly out of *Firenze*, consider taking the train to Pisa and flying out there. Make sure you adjust the days to the itinerary if you have taken any of the *Firenze* day trips. Now it's on to *Venezia* (Venice) as we say.

DAY 7- TRAIN TO VENICE

After an early morning breakfast at your hotel make your way back to *Firenze's* Santa Maria Novella *stazione* (SMN) where you arrived from *Roma*. Locate your train on the big electronic board. Don't panic if you don't see your train number yet. It usually posts about 20 minutes prior to departure. When it does display it will state the track i.e. the *bin*. Don't look for Venice on that big *partenze* board. You won't find it. It will instead say *Venezia*.

Once the *bin* is posted, make your way to that sleek train waiting to whisk you to Venice. You must locate the *carozza* number (car number) which corresponds to your ticket number on the electronic sign board on the rail car. Then board and make your way to your reserved seats. Once again, if you are in the wrong car, walk the train until you arrive in the correct car. Do not disembark the train to find your car. The train may pull out of the station without you!

Try to arrive at least forty minutes before train departure time to purchase some goodies at the station, as coffee, breakfast sandwiches and pastries sold on the train, are rather pricey. It's a few minutes over two hours on the high speed Trenitalia *Frecciarossa* or the *Frecciargento* (the *Frecci*) ETR train. These high speed trains operate every hour or two depending on the time of the day. Avoid taking any regional, sometimes called a local train. You may save ten Euros; however, it will take over four hours and you will waste an entire day.

>>>TIP<<<

As discussed prior, you should book these *Frecci* tickets before you leave the USA. It is best to book the train as soon as the 120 day window is posted to get the best train for your journey.

>>>>><<<<<

During your two hour journey the train passes mostly agricultural areas where grapes and wheat are grown. While the countryside is not as breathtaking as the *Bernina Express* (Chapter 7) it is certainly beautiful and serene. There are several tunnels as the train transits the Apennine Mountains which run the spine of Italy. You will pass by Bologna then enter the area of *Emila-Romana* and the Po River valley before stopping in Padua (*Padova*) for two minutes, home of St. Anthony's Basilica and the university.

A few minutes after leaving Padua the landscape turns into a flat marshy area as you approach *Venezia*. If you are sitting on the right hand side of the train you can get a nice view of the land which was probably all underwater a million years ago before the Adriatic Sea receded. In a few minutes you will arrive in Venice. Now here is a little information about Venice which few first time travelers don't know.

TWO SIDES OF VENICE

Did you know that there are two "sides" of Venice? That's right. Most people think of Venice as a place where there are no roads and only canals. This is true. However, there is another side of Venice which was created about AD 1152. It's the mainland side of

Venice as opposed to the lagoon. It's called Venice Mestre (pronounced *mes-stray*).

All trains stop at Venice Mestre before going the extra 12 minutes over the lagoon water's to Venice's Santa Lucia terminal. When you purchase your ticket to Venice Santa Lucia you can always get off the train at Venice Mestre. So best to buy your reserved seat ticket for Venice's Santa Lucia station via the *Frecci* type trains. It's usually the same price. Now the question is "should I stay in the lagoon or stay in Mestre?" Here are the pros and cons.

If you decide to stay in the lagoon, you will find it very romantic as opposed to staying in Mestre. If you are on your honeymoon, in my opinion, it's best to stay in the lagoon. There will be about 300 times more restaurants and hotels. Gondolas and all types of water boats will be scooting around the canals. Shops restaurants, cafes and the pigeons will be all over the place along with thousands of "wall-to-wall" people. Of utmost importance, if you are a history buff, are the churches, the *piazzas* (the squares) and the history of the lagoon.

You should expect to pay double or triple for a hotel room in the lagoon as opposed to staying in Venice

Mestre which is only a 12 minute train ride away. There are many hotels across from the train station, with a train every 20 minutes to Santa Lucia station at a cost of less than two Euros. My favorite is the Hotel Plaza Venice directly across from the Mestre train station. There are others. Once again, see Chapter 11.

>>>TIP<<<

If you do stay at the Hotel Plaza Venice, there is an excellent restaurant located about five blocks behind the hotel. Just ask the hotel front desk to make you a reservation at *Ristorante Da Bepi Venesian* and ask the hotel clerk to give you directions. It's simple to find, and it's so good I always eat there two times on every trip to *Venezia.* If you love fish and seafood, this is the place. Please give the brothers who own *Da Bepi* my best regards.

>>>><<<<<

Now, on the negative side, I have always found that staying in the lagoon is a logistical nightmare, however, once again it is romantic. Let me explain, but first a tutorial on the watercraft you will see.

WATER TRANSPORT VEHICLES

This may be confusing, so let me clear it up before I discuss the water transport vehicles in Venice: 1) *vaporetti*, 2) gondolas and 3) water taxis.

The *vaporetto* is also called a water bus. The plural for *vaporetto* is *vaporetti*. It is operated by the Venezia municipal transport agency known as ACTV. Vaporetto Lines 1 and 2 are the most popular as they ply the Grand Canal. Single tickets for riding for up to 75 minutes cost 7.50 Euros. You can go one stop or the entire length of the Grand Canal and come back as long as you do not exceed the 75 minute duration which is determined once you validate or frank your ticket just before boarding the water bus. *Vaporetti* do not go into the real small canals but do go into the larger canals feeding the Grand Canal. You can climb aboard with your bags and there is no additional charge. There are about 70 plus stops (total) on both sides of the Grand Canal. Stops are also made on the larger islands of Giudecca, Murano, Burano, Torcello, the cruise terminal and Lido.

Gondolas are those boats you have seen in numerous pictures of Venice. They are powered by a *gondolier* who uses a large paddle to move the boat around the canal. There is no actual motor. The *gondolier* wears a black and white striped shirt, black pants and usually a straw hat with a red ribbon. For safety reasons, gondolas are not allowed to go into the Grand Canal since waves made by passing boats (wakes) and *vaporetti* can "swamp" the gondola and cause it to sink; definitely not a good idea.

Water taxis are private small boats that are licensed to pick groups of people up at certain points along the Grand Canal and other points in Venice.   The group can be 1-16 people.   You can consult the listings on the internet. They are regulated and must charge you by the standard water taxi tariff.   You can make arrangements for them to pick you up and take you to other points in Venice or even to or from the Marco Polo Airport, where there is a dock.   Payment can usually be prepaid with a credit card when booking. Now let's see how we find our hotel in the lagoon or should I say the maze?

STAYING IN THE LAGOON

Once you arrive at the last stop of the rail line, Venice's Santa Lucia Station (it's actually a terminal) dis-embark your train and hail a porter if necessary. You will then pass through the terminal area with all those shops and restaurants. Then exit the station and go down a flight of stairs and you will be on the banks of the Grand Canal. Yup, lots of people taking photos here. Make sure you mind your bags. I always suggest a photo op here before you go down the balance of the steps to the Grand Canal. Just make sure you don't get knocked over by all those tourists! If you don't want to drag your bags down the twenty-plus steps, you will find a ramp in the far left corner of the train station before you take the main exit to the Grand Canal.

>>>TIP<<<

Suggest you take advantage of the facilities before departing the *stazione*. They are located on the far left hand side, next to the first track as you exit the track area. And yes, you will need a Euro to gain entrance. Have your travelling companion watch your bags.

>>>>><<<<<

Here comes the real challenge. You must make your way to your hotel. Not a big deal if you are in good physical shape. It's sort of an obstacle course, unless you are staying at one of the few hotels on the left as you exit the terminal where you can simply roll your bag along with you and check into your hotel. However, bear in mind that these hotels pick up a lot of noise from the cafes and the activity on the Grand

Canal. If staying at one of these hotels, do ask for a quiet room perhaps off the canal.

Now, if you are not checking into one of the hotels abutting the train station (see my listings in Chapter 11) there are basically four ways to find your hotel. The easiest way is to summon one of those porters at the base of the steps as you exit the station. They are easily spotted in their bright blue coveralls. These porters will take you and your bags to your hotel anywhere in the lagoon area. However, it tends to be pricey. Expect to pay 20-50 Euros (negotiable) for your porter and in addition you must also pay for his/her ticket on the *vaporetto* (waterbus) and also your tickets. If you are only a short distance from the station, he will walk you and take your bags usually over several bridges and find your hotel. All you need do is follow the porter. I have always found the use of a porter to be the best way to find your hotel if it is not easily reachable or accessible. It is best to pay the price and eliminate all that mental and physical stress. All the more needed if it's your honeymoon.

Another way to find your hotel is either to walk with your bag or take the *vaporetto* to the closest point to your hotel and then walk from there. I always suggest that you contact the hotel via email and ask them which is the closest *vaporetto* stop? *Vaporetto* numbers 1 and 2 depart directly in front of the Santa Lucia *stazione*. You must buy your tickets at the ACTV yellow and black ticket booth abutting the *vaporetto* stop. Check the *vaporetto* routes and easiest way before you get to the lagoon. Most of the time you will still have to drag your bags up and down those small bridges connecting the over 117 islands which make up the community of Venice. I might note supposedly there are over 400 bridges spanning 150 canals linking the islands in the lagoon. So be prepared to go up and down many steps. Oh, don't get scared when you see that large bridge over the Grand Canal to your left (*Scalzi* Bridge) when you exit the train station. There are only about a dozen of these monster bridges in Venice. Most of the smaller bridges tend to have 8-12 steps on each side. No question you will get a step aerobics workout locating your hotel. Be patient as you navigate the maze.

Another way to find your hotel is to hire your own private water taxi. This can be real pricey! It's like hiring a private car and driver or a limo. As discussed above, all the water taxis adhere to the tariff; most of the time you can locate this service on the internet. On arrival at the station, you call them and they will pick you up and take you to your hotel. Expect to pay

50-200 Euros per couple for this custom service depending on where your hotel is located in the lagoon. Just like a taxi, it is the same price for up to five people. After five people there is an additional charge per person. It definitely pays off for a group.

There are two more lodging areas to mention here. If it's the summertime when Venice is packed with visitors and you have several days to spare, consider a hotel on the Venice Lido or in a town called *Venice de Jesolo.*

Venice Lido is a barrier island about 20 minutes away by *vaporetto.* It protects the lagoon islands from the Adriatic Sea. Nice stately hotels can be found here, lots of restaurants and nice beaches (see below for more on the Lido). There are *vaporetti* every 30 minutes or so to the Lido from the St. Mark's (*San Marco*) area and the *Piazzale Roma* in the peak summer season. Outside of the peak season, if you take *vaporetto* number 1 or number 2 there is a chance you will probably have to connect with another *vaporetto* at one of the St. Mark's (*San Marco*) stops (there are two of them). It is best to consult an attendant at any one of the **ACTV** yellow and black ticket booths.

The *Venice de Jesolo* area is also another beach community about 20 miles from Venice reachable by waterbus from Venice's Santa Lucia station. *Venice de Jesolo* has numerous beach hotels. These are ideal for families and cost considerably less than staying in the lagoon, Mestre or on the Lido. There are lots of things for the family to do including the *Aqualandia* water-park and many places for family dining, all within walking distance of your hotel. In the summer season there is a ferry shuttle about every hour from *Venice de Jesolo* to the Grand Canal area. Throughout the year you can buy a combination bus and boat ticket. It is best to check ACTV, the regional transportation authority's website.

THE VENICE WALK

Once you have checked into your lagoon or Mestre hotel, I recommend what I call the Venice meander or walk. If you arrive at your hotel after 2 PM (14:00) I would strongly suggest you do the Venice Walk after breakfast on your second day in Venice. There will be more time for shopping and just taking your time instead of rushing to get back to your hotel. It would be best to visit the Peggy Guggenheim museum, the Duomo, The Dogi's Palace, St Mark's *Campanile* (the tower) or the Lido if the weather is really nice. Consult the internet for entrance fees and times of operation. Else, just spend the balance of the day at either the Rialto market area or San Marco's *Piazza.*

But before we do the walk, here is a quick note on Venice flooding. Yes, you read it correctly, Venice floods! Several times of the year depending on tides and other phenomenon, a high tide for Venice is forecast. The high water can last four hours or many days. Many of the main walking streets actually become flooded. This can be from two inches to almost a foot. The Municipality of Venice has an army of people who immediately place boardwalks over the flooded or potentially flooding areas to allow all the residents and tourists to walk the City without getting their shoes wet. The flooding does not have to occur when there is a thunderstorm or a rainy day—the place just floods even if the sun is out. Don't be shocked if you see the boardwalks being set up, you will still enjoy the walk without your shoes or sneakers being soaked. Now, let's do the walk.

This walk starts from the Santa Lucia train station and ends at San Marco's Piazza. There are numerous cafes, restaurants, shops and points of interest along the entire route. Be gracious—if you need to use the facilities you can always swing in to a bar or café, use the facilities and have a café! Suggest you order the café first! Also, once you arrive at the Rialto Bridge and market area there are public facilities. Make sure you have a few one Euro coins in your pocket because there is a charge to use the public facilities.

If you are doing the walk, it's easy to get lost in the Venice "maze". Trust me, it's a maze. If you become disoriented just look up at the corner of the building at any intersection and observe those black painted arrows pointing to St. Mark's (San Marco), Rialto, or the *Ferrovia* (Santa Lucia train station).

There are just a few key points here. Because the walk is about a mile and takes you over perhaps 12-20 bridges depending on your route, consider walking to St. Mark's via Rialto Bridge and market area and then taking either Number 1 or Number 2 *vaporetto* back to Santa Lucia *stazione* at the end of the day. Check with the ACTV ticket booth on your return, since Number 2 *vaporetto* has several return routes back to the *Ferrovia* (train station).

If you are somewhat physically challenged, or find that a long walk up and down bridges would be quite a considerable stress, consider taking the Number 1 vaporetto to the stop marked Rialto Mercato (note, this is not one of the regular Rialto stops which are across the canal). Getting off at Rialto Mercato will eliminate one of those monster bridges, the *Scalzi,* just to the left of the Santa Lucia rail station where you arrived. However, you must still walk the steps of the famous Rialto Bridge (another monster bridge) with its breathtaking views of the Grand Canal. Other than Rialto, this will be the only monster bridge you will encounter on your way to St. Mark's square. I believe there may be a few small bridges in your path. This should present no problem on your way to San Marco.

The *vaporetto* Number 1 is your best bet for viewing all those mansions (with those flooded basements) on the Grand Canal. Make sure you have your camera ready and do stand toward the front of the boat. Also now is the time to be real street savvy (even on a boat) and be careful with your handbags and carry-on.

You can also walk to the Rialto *Mercato.* Just cross that *Scalzi* bridge to the left of the train station and follow the signs to Rialto. You can also take a hard left on exiting the train station and follow the signs to Rialto without crossing the *Scalzi* bridge. But this is a long way to go and ultimately you will have to cross the canal with one of the "cross the canal" ferries or work your way to the **Rialto Bridge** and cross over to the Rialto *Mercato* that way.

Once you arrive at the **Rialto** market area, a/k/a just "Rialto", you will find many street vendors selling everything from fruits and vegetables to leather belts, scares and all that other good stuff you want to bring back so you can wrap it up and place it under the Christmas tree! You will also see all this other stuff in the St. Mark's area. So if you don't want to carry it around with you, don't worry, you will have a second time to buy it all when you get to St. Mark's.

Depart the Rialto market area by climbing the 30 plus steps to the top of the **Rialto Bridge** for some great photo ops overlooking the Grand Canal. Many travelers here will take your picture with a backdrop of the Grand Canal. So just keep your selfie-stick in your day bag. Hold your camera tightly on the Bridge. If you drop it, you won't see it again. Visit the shops if you wish on the bridge then work your way down the bridge to the other side.

Once on the other side you must go right and follow the crowds around the church. Follow the signs to St. Mark's (San Marco). Just a note, if you accidently go left at the bottom of the bridge you will find yourself in a maze! So make sure you make that right.

It's about a quarter mile walk to Piazza San Marco (St. Mark's Square) pretty much over flat narrow streets. If you are strolling, you should reach the *Piazza* in about 15 minutes or so. On arrival at San Marco you will be met with hordes and hordes of people and a lot of the local residents—the pigeons.

You can consult all the other tour books on what to do in St. Mark's *Piazza*. Of critical importance here is to watch out for the pigeons, especially when they are practicing their aerial bombardments.

Also, in the *Piazza* San Marco and the area where the gondolas depart next to the *Zaccaria vaporetto* stop, on the *Riva degli Schiavoni*, you will notice lots and lots of outdoor cafes in front of the five star hotels. Be prepared to spend at least $25 for two beers or two glasses of wine. Suggest you consult the menu before being seated. Menus are usually posted on a stand directly in front of the table area.

GONDOLA RIDES

If you can muster up two other couples to go on a 40 minute gondola ride, it will be worth the experience. It is best to stand in front of the gondola parking area, directly in front of the Danieli Hotel next to the *Zaccaria vaporetto* stop and just wait for another two couples who want to join you.

They usually charge about 80 Euros (cash only) for a gondola ride for the entire group of six people. If you want to go on a solo gondola ride (without anyone else) it will also cost you 80 Euros. The gondola holds eight people. Don't expect the "gondola driver" to sing *Oh Solo Meo*. They sing this only in Napoli. However, they do wear those colorful outfits of black and white stripes and red hats, great for a photo op, and yes the *gondoliers* do accept tips.

>>>TIP<<<

After taking a gondola ride, consider having lunch (*pranza*) at one of my favorite places, only one block behind the gondola parking area. It's called *Taverna dei Dogi* and it's right below the B&B named *Ca' dei Dogi*, located right on *Calle degli Albanesi*. Here you will find excellent seafood and pasta at popular prices.

>>>>><<<<<

After you are all shopped out, had lunch and taken that optional gondola ride, and your feet are really aching you can either walk back to your lagoon hotel or work your way back to the Santa Lucia *stazione* for your train back to Venice Mestre. To get back to Mestre, all you need do is follow those little black arrows marked *Ferrovia* (literally means way of the steel) on the corners of those old buildings which will direct you back to the Santa Lucia *stazione*.

If you are going back to the Santa Lucia *stazione*, go to the yellow and black ACTV floating ticket booth and buy your tickets for a *vaporetto* number 1 or number 2 back to the train station. Make sure you get the *vaporetto* going in the correct direction and do always ask the attendant on board or the ticket taker if the *vaporetto* will make your stop i.e. the *stazione* or *Ferrovia*. Make sure you have your camera ready. Also, like the trains, you must also validate or frank your *vaporetto* ticket before getting on board the waterbus. Failure to do so is a fine.

Depending on time of day, *vaporetto* number 2 zigs and zags on the Grand Canal before entering the cruise ship terminal, then continuing to the *Plaza d Roma* and the *stazione*.

Once you reach the *stazione* stop, disembark the *vaporetto*, climb the stairs (attendants will help you) and enter the Santa Lucia terminal. Check the departure board for any regional train departing in the next 15 minutes. All regional trains will stop at Mestre. Then validate your ticket at the yellow or green machines on the platform and hop aboard any regional train, not the intercity trains which have reserved seats! Best is to also ask the train conductor if the train stops in Mestre. Remember to get off at Venice Mestre (which is usually the first stop, though some trains stop at Marghera), else you will find yourself in Padua or Trieste!

After exiting the Mestre train station, cross the street and work your way back to your Mestre area hotel.

VENICE EXTRA DAYS

If you are planning another day in Venice, my suggestions are to either visit the islands of Murano for the glass making and or Burano for its linen making. Time permitting; a visit to the Peggy Guggenheim Museum is also worth a few hours. Consider also the Lido. This is a barrier island, home to almost 100 beautiful hotels and B&Bs, with many of them facing the beach or lagoon. Many places on the Lido are closed outside of the summer season or at least from November through April.

THE LIDO

Vaporetti depart from St. Mark's and the Plaza d' Roma for about a twenty minute ride to the Lido. Check with **ACTV** for other departure points depending on time of year. The entire Lido is easy to enjoy, since it is all flat and delightfully walk-able. The main boulevard is the *Gran Viale Santa Maria Elisabetta*. It is lined with numerous cafes, restaurants and gelato shops. You should plan on spending an afternoon here for lunch and shopping after a morning visit to the Peggy Guggenheim museum or another attraction you can visit in about two hours.

MURANO, BURANO AND TORCELLO

There are two ways to get to the island of Murano. You can catch a *vaporetto #3—Diretto* Murano, which makes the run in **17** minutes or the *vaporetto* number **4.1**, which is slower since it makes several stops. Like all the *vaporetti*, there is a fee involved. However, several glass making shops offer free transfers to and from the lagoon area for a complimentary visit to their businesses to see how they blow the glass. Hopefully, you will buy some of these beautiful works of art. It is best to check on line or with your hotel's concierge.

Also, there are several local tour operators who will take you for the day to Murano, Burano and Torcello. It is best again to make an enquiry with your concierge or consult the internet.

Once you complete your one or two full days in Venice, you can either fly home from Venice or continue to Milan for several days in the Lakes District and either take the *Bernina Express* to Switzerland or explore the Swiss Alps with the *Glacier Express*. All of these options follow.

If you are going directly to Venice's Marco Polo Airport (VCE), you can take a bus from Mestre or a taxi. If departing from the lagoon area you need to work your way over to the *Piazzale Roma* (just say *Piazza Roma*). Taxi fares run about 35-50 Euros from either Mestre or the *Piazzale Roma*. Buses operated by ACTV (the AeroBus) also depart *Piazza Roma* for the airport. There are about three per hour and the cost is about seven Euros. And yes, there is one more way to reach Marco Polo Airport. You can hire a water taxi which will take you from your lagoon hotel directly to the airport. However, these water taxis start at a minimum of 100 Euros. Some of them will take as many as ten people.

There is no train service as of yet to the Venice Marco Polo Airport from either the lagoon area or Mestre. If you are continuing your rail trip to Milan and the Lakes District and possibly over the Alps on the *Bernina Express* with a fly home from Zurich airport, read on.

CHAPTER 6

MILAN & THE LAKES DISTRICT

ITINERARY B

MILAN & LAKES ROUGH OUT:

Day 1- ETR (*Frecci*) fast train from Venice to
Milano *Centrale* or fly into Milan (MXP)
Sightseeing in Milan

Day 2- Day trip to Lake Maggiore

Day 3- Day trip to Lake Como

Day 4- Day trip to Lake Lugano

Day 5- Fly home from Milan
-or continue over the Alps
with the *Bernina Express*
-or to Venice, Rome, and Florence
if you are starting you trip in Milan

Note: There are four nights in Milan preferably
in one of the hotels around the Milano
Centrale train station.

The Lakes District abuts the Italian/Swiss Alps and lies to the north of an imaginary line you can draw from Venice to Turin. The southern portion of much of the lakes lies in the Po River Valley, while the northern sections lie at the foot of the Alps.

Many lakes give the Lakes District its name. However, travelers to this region known as Piedmont and Lombardy usually mean the lakes of Maggiore, Como and Lugano, although Garda also makes the list. There are other lakes; however, for the purposes of this book I only discuss the three most notable and visited lakes: Maggiore, Como and Lugano.

These lakes are massive in terms of European standards. But don't compare them to our Great Lakes. In fact, Como alone is about 30 miles long and two miles wide. You can spot it on a map of Italy because it is an inverted "Y." The lakes in the Lakes District were formed after the last glacial ice age.

All three of the lakes are my favorites and all are worth visiting for the day, if not several days.

The Lakes District can be visited either of two ways. You can continue your itinerary from Venice by taking a high speed train known as the Red Arrow or   in

Italian *Frecciarossa* (yes, the F*recci*) to the capital of Italy's north—Milan. This high speed train, equivalent to the TGV trains of France, makes the trip between Venice's Santa Lucia station and Milan's *Centrale* (main train station) in about two hours. It's the equivalent of driving by car about 166 miles. With stops, this would take you 3-4 hours. The fare also is certainly worth it, averaging about 20 Euros in second class coach.

Another way to enjoy the Lakes District and the region known as *Lombardia* and the Piedmont is to start your Italy vacation by flying into Milan instead of Rome and reversing your itinerary. In other words, you take the train to Venice after you explore Milan and the Lakes District. You then continue your rail trip from Venice to Florence and then on to Rome.

The three major lakes worth visiting are Maggiore, Como and Lugano. I might note that Lugano (not Lucano) is partly in Italy (about one third) and partly in Switzerland (about two thirds). The actual city of Lugano is in Switzerland, so it's best to remember to make sure you have your passports with you since Switzerland is sometimes part of the European Union (EU) and sometimes not part of the EU. It's an odd situation with the EU and beyond the scope of this book. However, this may change in the future. So best to be safe if you are an American and carry your passport with you, which by the way is a law for all non-Italian citizens; so much for Lugano.

Details follow on each lake, how to get there and what to see. You should plan on a full day to see the most popular towns on each lake. Plan to depart from *Centrale* about 9:30 AM and return about 7 PM (19:00).

Each of the three lakes can be visited in any order. However, in the summer, on Sundays, there are eight hour excursions out of the city of Como which tour Lake Como. However, the city of Como is not the jumping off place to see Bellagio and Varenna, both on Lake Como, unless you are taking that eight hour cruise from the city of Como. The city of Como is reached on the Lugano rail line with regional as well as high speed intercity trains bound for Zurich which require reserved seats.

If you have more time to spend on any one lake consider Maggiore. This is my favorite of my three favorites, because it is home to the Borromean Islands located about 10 minutes into the lake from either Stresa or Baveno. All you need do is check out of your hotel in Milan one day earlier, tell the hotel to hold your bags and pack an overnight bag where you can either overnight in Stresa or Baveno. This will allow you two days to visit the highlights of this lake. You then return to your Milan hotel, pickup your bags and head for Venice via rail or Zurich via the *Bernina Express*; more on Stresa below.

MILANO *CENTRALE* AS A BASE

The modus operandi for visiting the Lakes District and Milan itself is to base yourself in a hotel no more than a 10 minute walk, say no more than six city blocks from the main train station Milano *Centrale*. In fact, there are literally over 100 hotels in this area.

My favorite is a four star hotel only three blocks away on a quiet side street—the Hotel Colombia. It's a four-star boutique hotel with a breakfast of almost a five star hotel. Best to book direct via email to the hotel. Oh, and by the way, if you get one of the smaller rooms, do inform the manager and perhaps they can upgrade you to a larger room. Also, it is best to request a room overlooking the courtyard as opposed to the street since there is usually less noise.

You will find additional hotels around Milano *Centrale* in Chapter 11. There are also numerous eating establishments in the area and in *Centrale*.

You will need five days in Milan for the Lakes District (and Milan) if you are beginning your itinerary in Milan, since you need at least a day just to recover from the jet lag. It's best to recover in Milan where you can visit the world famous Duomo Cathedral of Milan in the afternoon or evening after you "snooze" off your overnight flight. It's best not to attempt any trip to one of the lakes on your arrival in Milan. So, just take it easy for the day.

If you are not flying into Milan but instead taking the train from Venice, you may want to depart on a train, about 10 AM. This will put you at your hotel about noon, enough time to visit The Cathedral of Milan. If you are arriving on a Saturday, consider an earlier train so you arrive at your hotel about 10 AM in time for the major street fair (on *Alessandro Tadino*) about ten blocks from Milano *Centrale*. Once you check your bags at the hotel and grab a café, you can stroll down to the street fair and shop, shop, shop.

You can certainly tour all three lakes if you wish by taking trains to each lake, checking into a hotel and wasting about one half day. In addition, you will have to lug your bags. I might note that you will have to go back and forth to Milan each time you wish to go to another lake because there are no trains which take you lake to lake! I have always found that if you are going to "rail it", it's best to base yourself in Milan and take the trains to the three main towns of the lakes. The trains make the run in about one hour and cost 10-24 Euros round trip. Because Lugano is in Switzerland, fares are higher. Thousands of people each day take the trains from Milan to the lakes and return in the late afternoon or the evening to *Centrale*.

Now, for those starting their rail tour by flying into Milan, you are best to fly into Milan's Malpensa Airport (MXP) which has rail service to *Centrale*. If you fly into Milan's Linate (LIN) Airport, you will have to take a bus to Milan's *Centrale* (Central) train terminal since there is no rail service. Buses depart every half hour for the 25 minute ride to *Centrale*. The cost varies but is less than five Euros per person. For more info see the websites *atm.it* or *autostradale.it*. Either way you will get to *Centrale*.

Trains from Milan's Malpensa airport (The Malpensa Express) depart every 20 minutes for the 50 minute ride to Milano *Centrale*. The fare is 13 Euros. Make sure your train is bound for Milano *Centrale* and not *Cadorma* which is a shorter ride by about 20 minutes. However, once at *Cadorma* you have to take the Milan subway *Metropolitana di Milano* to *Centrale*. So best just to take the direct Malpensa Express to *Centrale*. Do make sure you validate your ticket at the yellow or green machine near the *BIN* (platform) and do watch your bags and carry-on items on the train. The *Malpensa Express* departs and arrives at Terminal 1 at MXP. There is a free shuttle from Terminal 2.

Milano *Centrale* is one of the largest train stations in Europe, (actually it's a terminal). Compared to notable stations in the United States i.e. New York's Pennsylvania and Grand Central Station and Chicago's Union Station, *Centrale* is overwhelming. You could probably drop Pennsylvania and Grand Central Station into *Centrale* and still have enough room left over to drop in Chicago's Union Station. That's the size of *Centrale*. Opened in 1931, it serves 120 million passengers a year. On a given day over 500 trains arrive and depart *Centrale*. If you have nothing to do for several hours consider exploring the three levels of this magnificent piece of architecture and its beautiful artwork within.

Centrale consists of three levels connected by numerous escalators and elevators. Trains depart and arrive on the top level, *binaria* or track level. There are numerous cafés, restaurants and take-away shops on each level. You should note that there are no facilities on the track level. You must go down one level to *Piano Ammezzanto*, and do remember to have one Euro in your pocket for the "turn-style".

At *Centrale* you purchase your tickets for Trenitalia, Trenord or Italo on the ground level (*Terra Level*) where you enter the station. Avoid using the machines to purchase tickets. I find them intimidating. All agents usually speak English and will suggest discounts i.e. "are you a senior and would you like a discount or would you like an open return ticket?" If you are taking the Lugano day trip and using an Intercity high speed train (the *Frecci*) you can use only your Eurail pass (not the Eurail Italy or the Eurail Swiss pass) but you must visit the counter of the railway company to obtain your seat reservations (extra charge). See the entire chapter on the Eurail pass since in most cases you will not save any money with an Italy Eurail pass. Now here are the details on each lake and how to get there from *Centrale*.

LAKE MAGGIORE

The main town of Lake Maggiore is Stresa, which is on the western side of the lake. Baveno is a smaller town with many hotels about four miles north of Stresa. Both towns offer ferry service operated by the government-owned *Navigazione Lago Maggiore* to the Borromean Islands which are located less than one mile east of the lake shore from Stresa and about one mile south of Baveno. Visiting these islands is what you do when you visit Stresa.

Stresa deserves two days if you have the time, since there are other things to do there. So best to pack an overnight bag and check your bags with the bellman of your hotel, or just leave your bags in your room and pay that extra night instead of having to pack-up, check the bags then check-in again and unpack.

In addition to the Borromean Islands, Stresa is also known for the Ernest Hemingway novel *"A Farewell to Arms"* (original novel 1929 by Scribner).

The story goes like this. In the middle of a stormy and rainy night in November, 1918, in the final days of World War I, Frederic Henry, (Ernest Hemingway); and his pregnant lover Catherine, row 21 miles across

121

Lake Maggiore from Stresa to neutral Switzerland to escape arrest by the Italian Army for insubordination. Prior to that rowing exercise across the lake, Hemingway meets up with Catherine and they spend a few nights at the Grand Hotel des Iles Borromees in Stresa before they decide to flee.

Getting to Stresa is quite easy. Regional as well as intercity trains depart *Centrale* every hour or two and make the journey to Stresa in about an hour. The round trip fare is about 20 Euros.

You should avoid taking the train to Baveno even though there is ferry service to the Borromean Islands, because all trains to Baveno from *Centrale* require a change of trains at Domodossola or Verbania-Pallanza and take over two hours for the journey. So, it is best to go directly to Stresa. You can visit Baveno with the lake ferry service since ferries operate from Baveno to the islands as well as to Stresa.

>>>TIP<<<

You can still overnight in Baveno instead of Stresa if you wish. Take the train to Stresa and a taxi for about 15 Euros to Baveno. You can also take the ferry from Stresa to Baveno. It is about 10 minutes. Best hotel to stay at, is the Grand Hotel Dino. It's a four star hotel directly on the lake and truly elegant. The ferry to the Borromean Islands and Stresa is next to the hotel. If you have one night to spend in the Stresa area and wish to stay in Baveno, this is the place. I have personally stayed at the "Dino" and would definitely go back. It is right on the lake and having breakfast or dinner there is breath-taking.

On exiting the Stresa station, it is a short walk to the ferry terminal for your 10 minute boat ride to the Islands. Be careful. It's easy to get lost in Stresa! The town is one big maze! Here is what you need to do:

As you exit the station, walk to your right about a block or two until you spot *Via Duchessa di Genova.* There should be a traffic light here, as it is a main boulevard. Go down the street with your back toward the rail line. About five blocks down you will come to the lake. Go right when you see the wide boulevard next to the shore. This is the *Corso Italia.* The ferry terminal (*traghetti*) is about three blocks on your left.

Combination tickets, 5-10 Euros each, are sold for two island or three island visits. Before buying tickets, do enquire about the senior discounts. Ticket booths accept all major credit cards. Ferries run between

Stresa (also Baveno) and the islands every twenty minutes so if you miss one there will be another shortly. In addition, you do not have to go back to Stresa to visit the other islands. There is inter-island service. Just ask the attendants wearing the white caps or make an enquiry at the ticket booth while enjoying your gelato.

Of the three Borromean Islands, the Isola Madre is not inhabited but worth the visit if you have extra time or you are staying overnight in Stresa or Baveno. It's inhabited with peacocks and has a lovely botanical garden in addition to a smaller Borromean Palace. You will have to purchase a three island combo ticket to visit Isola Madre in addition to the two other islands i.e., Isola Superiore-Pescatori and Isola Bella with its lovely palace and gardens known as the Palazzo Borromeo. Also, because not many people visit Isola Madre, ferry service can be quite spotty, i.e. a ferry every hour.

The other two islands are definitely worth the visit and will require about two hours each. Add another two hours if you will be having lunch at one of the many restaurants and cafes on both islands. I might note that both islands have small hotels and bed and breakfasts, if you wish to stay overnight here instead of Stresa or Baveno.

Isola Pescatore and Isola Bella are quite small. You can actually walk around each island in less than 15 minutes. Don't expect any type of taxis or buses to be plying the streets. There aren't any streets! Both islands have a main walkway around the island and are dotted with lots of restaurants, cafes, souvenir shops and small hotels. There are several public facilities on each island and they are quite clean. However, make sure you have that one Euro coin in your pocket!

Isola Bella is special. It is home to the Palace of the Borromeos and its beautiful gardens. Once on the island, find your way to the entry to the palace (lots of steps here) and purchase your tickets. And yes, they will take your credit cards again.

So, now it's about 4 PM or 5 PM (17:00) and you are "pooped" from walking all day. Yup, those two islands were enough! Board your ferry back to Stresa (note, you are not going to Baveno) and head for the Grand Hotel des Iles Borromees for a drink before going back to Milano. The hotel is over 100 years old and is definitely grand. Have a seat in the lounge, sip your favorite drink or even a glass of Perrier and just remember you could be sitting where Hemingway and Catherine sat almost 100 years ago!

The Grand Hotel des Iles Borromees is about four blocks to the right of the ferry terminal facing the shore. Also, if you are not just pooped but really bushed, then consider taking a taxi to the station for about five Euros.

If you are planning on spending the night in Stresa, there are about one hundred hotels and B&Bs in this lovely town. Baveno, reached by the island ferries has also many hotels only a short walk from the ferry terminal. However, if you are heading to Baveno for the night, best to take a taxi since it will be faster and cost less for a couple.

On your second day here consider going on the tram known as *Funivia* Stresa Mottarone. It's a cable car. The views from the top of the mountain allow you to see most of Lake Maggiore and the nearby Alps of Switzerland.

In any case, make your way back to the Stresa *stazione* and head back to Milano *Centrale*. Make sure your train is heading to Milan and not Switzerland!

LAKE COMO

Of all the lakes in the lakes district, Como is my second favorite. And, no, it's not because George Clooney has a home here! Like its sister Lake Maggiore, its creation also dates from the last Ice Age. The lake is about 29 miles long by two miles wide at its widest point. The lake is actually an inverted Y. At the bottom of the "Y" in the western corner is the city of Como; on the eastern corner is the town of Lecco. The right and left legs of the lake start to diverge at the town of Bellagio, which of course is surrounded by water to the east and west.

Como is the third largest lake in Italy and one of the largest lakes in Europe. It is 660 feet below sea level. This is quite deep compared with California's Death Valley which is only 282 feet below sea level. The depth of the lake varies but at its deepest point it reaches 1300 feet below the surface. For many miles the lake is surrounded by granite mountains which drop shear down to the lake's surface thus eliminating any lake shore where a boat can moor or one can get off, fish or lay on the beach.

Within a few miles of the snow covered Italian and Swiss Alps, the two major resort towns of Bellagio and Varenna enjoy a tropical climate. Both towns are home to numerous mansions and estates of the jet setters including yes, George Clooney.

There are only two ways to get to Lake Como via rail. On Sundays (consult the time table) you can take an entire eight hour tour of Lake Como from the city of Como. This is on the rail line to Lugano, Switzerland, which is also the rail line to Chiasso, Italy. This is not the same rail line as Varrena which is the gateway to Bellagio. So make sure you purchase the correct ticket and board the train bound for Tirano, not Chiasso or Lugano.

If you are going to take the Sunday eight hour cruise of Lake Como which makes several stops, you need to go to the city of Como. The train will be bound for Chiasso, Lugano or Zurich. Just make sure your train will stop in Como. Once arriving at the *San Giovanni stazione* in the city of Como, you will need to take a taxi for about a mile to the ferry terminal. It's a 20-30 minute walk. However, if you are short on time and want to make that eight hour cruise on the lake, best to spend the seven Euros and take the taxi. You should arrive about 30 minutes before cruise departure time.

There are other cruises from the city of Como; consult *comoanditslake.com* or *lakecomonavigation.htm.*

Also bear in mind that many day cruises may not allow enough time for shopping before you return to the city of Como. As an alternative consider a narrated tour of the lake from the city of Como to Bellagio. Then take the local ferry from Bellagio to Varenna. At Varenna take the train back to *Centrale.*

Varenna and Bellagio make a real nice day trip. There is no rail service to Bellagio. However, once arriving at the train station at Varenna (actually called *Varenna-Esino*), you merely take a short walk, all downhill of about 15 minutes to the Varenna ferry terminal and then board a ten minute ferry to Bellagio. All you need to do is follow the herd of tourists down to the lake. If you do not want to walk, there are taxis at the station which will take you down to the ferry terminal for about five Euros.

I would strongly suggest getting up to Varenna-Esino by 11 AM. See the local sights and have lunch before going over to Bellagio about 2 PM (14:00) for the rest of the afternoon and treating yourself to a gelato.

Trenord trains (part of Trenitalia) depart *Centrale* every hour for the one hour ride to *Varenna-Esino,* which is on the Tirano line. Make sure you purchase your tickets about 45 minutes prior to departure and do advise the counter person if you are a senior. The tickets are open seating and you can purchase them with an open return. Fares run about 15 Euros round trip per person. This is a regional train.

As soon as your train number is posted with the destination of Tirano (or Chiasso or Lugano, if you are going to the city of Como to take the cruise on the lake) you should proceed through security and find your *binaria* (*bin* or track). Ask someone on the train or one of the train conductors: "is this the train to Varenna or (Chiasso or Lugano which stops at Como)?" to make sure you are on the correct train. Make sure you get on the correct coach as some are first class only. Many of the new regionals have split cars with first class on one end and second class on the other. You may walk through the coaches once on the train. Remember to watch your personal belongings.

>>>TIP<<<

If you are taking the train to Varenna-Esino, see if you can get seats on the left side of the train. This will give you a view of the lake once you depart Lecco.
>>>>><<<<<

I won't steal the thunder from most of the travel books about Varenna and Bellagio. However, here are a few of my thoughts since you will usually have about 2-3 hours at each town.

Varenna has two important walkways which are right up against the lake. Many photos have been taken here. They are the Lover's Walk and the lakeside promenade in the center of the old *borgo* (the old town). The latter is filled with numerous cafes where you can enjoy lunch. There may not be enough time to visit any of the villas, mansions and gardens unless you plan on spending the night here or in Bellagio before returning to Milan the next day.

After lunch consider visiting Bellagio. Ferries depart about every 20 minutes for the ten minute run to Bellagio. Round trip fare is about seven Euros.

Once in Bellagio, consider taking the 30 minute tram tour of the highlights of the neighboring area of the town. The fare is five Euros (cash only) and is narrated in English. There are no stops, so consider using the facilities on the ferry from Varenna or at the ferry terminal on arrival in Bellagio. The 30 minute tram tour runs every 30 minutes so if you miss this one, the next will be along shortly.

Also, if you are considering spending the night in Bellagio, bear in mind that many B&Bs and hotels are reachable only by small paths with many steps. So do pack extra light, else you will be huffing and puffing and getting a good workout finding your overnight accommodations.

Just a quick note; on your return to Varenna to catch the train back to *Centrale*, make sure you get the correct ferry as ferries depart Bellagio for several towns on the lake. You want the ferry back to Varenna!

Under no circumstances board any ferry at Bellagio and head for the western shore or Cadenabbia. There is absolutely no rail service there. If you cannot get a ferry back to Varenna, there is always a private boat you can hire which will get you back to Varenna. The cost is about 20 Euros.

On arrival at Varenna from Bellagio you will have to walk up hill to reach the *stazione*. This is the same hill you walked down if you came by train from *Centrale* in the morning. You may want to consider taking a taxi from the ferry terminal for about five Euros.

It's about a one hour ride back to *Centrale*, perfect for snoozing. Don't worry about missing your stop, *Centrale* is the end of the line.

Now let's get on to Switzerland and Lake Lugano. But, first some information on Switzerland.

A NOTE ABOUT SWITZERLAND

Switzerland is totally an odd-ball country. During WWI and WWII they remained neutral. They are now part of the European Union. However, they abstain from several of the rules. They have strong immigration rules. They check passports sometimes on trains and other times they don't. But the biggest issue I have seen is that they insist on using their own currency which is the Swiss franc. Not a big deal. As of this writing, the Swiss franc was worth about the same as the Euro.

Switzerland brags about their standard of living. So let me see if I can explain this. A take-away meal in

Zurich will cost you $20, which in the US, Italy or the UK would be no more than $10. So everything costs about twice as much as you would expect to pay. However, that person serving you the take-away meal gets about the equivalent of $40,000 a year! This is also true for the cashier at the local supermarket. She gets about $50,000 per year. However, when she buys a loaf of plain old white bread it costs her $5! No big deal you say, since everything is in proportion. However, if you are arriving from Italy, your Euro will be worth about half in terms of purchasing power. So expect to pay twenty-five Euros for scrambled eggs (with hash browns and toast of course), for breakfast at your hotel. This does not include coffee which you can figure $5-6. I might note some items you may find on par. In summary, Switzerland is only expensive if you come into the country from some other country. The Swiss don't find it expensive, they live there!

LAKE LUGANO

The City of Lugano (not Lucano) is actually in Switzerland. It is located in the canton (province) of Ticino in one of the southern most points of Switzerland bordering Italy. It lies between Lake Maggiore and Lake Como. I don't know the history of the rail service here, but I can only believe that because of the predominate Italian speaking population, and the fact that it is on the border with Italy, the Italian rail system decided to make it the end of the line.

Getting there is quite easy. However in this writer's opinion it is pricy compared to the other lakes. Trains leave *Centrale* bound for Lugano (same line as the city of Como, not the Tirano line) about every other hour. The fare one way is twenty-four Euros. So you can see just the rail portion for the day for a couple will cost you about 100 Euros. Yes, Switzerland is costly and, most inter-country fares are much higher than point-to-point fares within Italy. High speed (ICs, known as inter-city) trains usually bound for Zurich, Switzerland, make the run in about one hour and fifteen minutes. All of these trains usually have reserved seats. Regional trains which may take a little longer do not usually have reserved seats. When purchasing the tickets at *Centrale* usually the day before, do ask for the senior discount and check if there is a special with a one day return.

Usually tickets for reserved seats do not require validation. However, it is best to just validate them if you can get them in the machine. As a tourist, don't panic if you forget to validate your ticket. I did it twice last fall on regional trains. Just claim you are a tourist and you just forgot. The train conductor will take your ticket and initial it and if he smiles you are okay. And remember, if you are on a regional train with un-reserved seats, you *must* validate or frank your ticket in the yellow or green machine on the platform.

WHAT TO DO IN LUGANO

Now the details of Lake Lugano: Yes, like Lake Maggiore and Como, Lugano was also formed during the last ice age during what is known as the Pleistocene Epoch. Supposedly this started about 2.5 million years ago and ended about 12,000 years ago. This was the most recent ice age. To put things in perspective, the dinosaurs disappeared about 60 million years before this last ice age. So, the formation of Lake Lugano as well as the other lakes in the district is quite new.

Like Como and Maggiore, Lugano also has a Mediterranean climate with palm trees and other tropical plants dotting the landscape even though it lies less than six miles from the snow covered Italian and Swiss Alps. The lake is named after the city of

Lugano. An interesting fact is that a good part of the lake lies in Italy, in the province of Lombardy.

Trains arrive at the central train station, yes, in Italian *stazione*, even though you are in Switzerland! There is not too much here since the station is located on a hill above the city. If you are going on to Zurich, by train from Lugano and not going via the *Bernina Express*, consider staying at the Continental Park Hotel, about one block from the station. The Continental Park Hotel located next to a park is a three star highly rated hotel. The author has personally stayed there. Best is to check your bags if your room is not ready, and head for the city and the lake.

To get to the city, you exit the platform and follow the pedestrian walkway through the tunnel toward the funicular or *funivia* in Italian. This will take you to the lower city where you will be greeted with an enormous open air market of shops selling everything from pastries and cheese to butchers selling chicken and cuts of beef. The lower station of the *funivia* is located on Piazza Cioccaro.

If you have checked into the Continental Park Hotel, you must walk back to the station and take the funicular to the lower city.

There are loads of hotels within walking distance of the *funivia*; however, bear in mind that you will have to lug your bags on the *funivia* or locate a hard to find porter. Remember if you are going on to Zurich, you will also have to do all in reverse since the station is atop the city or else take a taxi for a few Euros.

From the train station and the Continental Park Hotel, which sit high on the hill, you can take breathtaking pictures of Lake Lugano with the Swiss Alps as a backdrop.

There are many things to do in Lugano. Here are my suggestions for the day: This is a place to shop, shop, and shop some more. Stroll the small streets and just take in the pastel buildings and the beauty of the architecture. Visit the *Piazza della Riforma* with its dozens of bistros and cafes. It's only an eight minute walk from the base of the *funivia*.

Grab a sandwich (best at the base of the *funivia*) or just buy some cold cuts and a loaf of some crusty bread (and don't forget a bottle of wine) at one of the many shops; and work your way over to the *Parco Civico* for a picnic lunch. This park is gorgeous with breathtaking views of the lake.

138

If it's a hot summer day, head for the *Lido di Lugano*, which is a public beach on the lake. Note, the water may be very cold, even in the summer! The Lido also has heated swimming pools, a diving pool and volleyball fields.

Now, if you get to Lugano early, about **11 AM** you might want to consider a morning boat tour of the lake. Tours operate year round. However there are more tours from April through September. It is best to check with The Navigation Company of Lake Lugano, *lakelugano.ch/en.*

After your morning boat tour, feel free to enjoy a picnic lunch or lunch at many of the cafes on the *Piazza della Riforma.*

About **5 PM (17:00)** get that train back to Milano *Centrale*, enjoy dinner and get ready for your flight back to the USA from either Malpensa or Linate airports in Milan. If you are continuing on to Switzerland via the *Bernina Express* (Itinerary C) over the Alps to Switzerland skip the departure instructions below from Milan airports and read on to the next chapter—Over the Alps on the *Bernina Express.*

MILAN— AN EXTRA DAY

While Milan is very much the capital city of northern Italy, it is also the capital city for the province of Lombardy. Milan is the hub of finance, banking and manufacturing, and is the home of Italy's stock exchange. The city is only second to Rome in population. When people think of Milan, they think of fashion. It is, indeed, one of the fashion capitals of the world. There is much to see in Milan. However, it would take you a month at a minimum to just scratch the surface. My suggestions are the absolute musts. As an aside, you may want to consider the Milan hop-on-hop-off bus which will give you a good orientation of the city and its highlight's. Here are the top sights:

A must visit is the Duomo of Milan, also called the Cathedral of Milan. Unlike St. Peter's in the Vatican, which is of Roman and Greek design, the Duomo of Milan is Gothic and extremely ornate, with numerous spires on all sides. It is the largest church in Italy (St. Peter's is in the Vatican) and the third largest in Europe. It took 600 years to build. And yes, like St. Peter's you can take an elevator to the top of the church (the roof) for the view or climb those steps.

Another sight worth visiting is the *Galleria Vittorio Emanuele II*. This was destroyed when the Allies bombed Milan during WWII. After the war it was rebuilt. Now it's an indoor shopping mall believed to be one of the oldest in the western world. In fact, it's over one hundred years old. But the real attraction of this mall is its architecture. The ceiling is made up of glass domes and arches, thus letting the natural light in. The *Galleria* is home to numerous designer shops, restaurants and a hotel.

Something different to be considered is the *Sforza Castle Museum*. Yes, it's a former castle, but a big one. It's medieval in nature and even has a moat around it, like the *Tower of London*. It now houses about ten different museums and it also happens to be only a few blocks from the *Santa Maria delle Grazie* church, which houses Da Vinci's *The Last Supper*.

Oh, I almost forgot. If you are into opera, don't forget the *La Scala Opera* house. Make sure you purchase tickets in the USA when planning your trip. Also, check out their museum which is open daily (check schedule on line) and is about ten Euros for entry. There website is *eatroallascala.org/* and it's quite easy to find from the Metropolitana Yellow line stop. Please see below.

THE METROPOLITANA DI MILANO

Like Rome, Milano has its own very modern subway system called the ATM (not to be confused with a *Bancomat* ATM machine). Hopefully, if your hotel is located a few blocks from the Milano *Centrale* rail station, you have it made. The Yellow and the Green line interchange at a subway station directly in front of Milano *Centrale* and of course it's named *Centrale*.

The ATM includes four subway lines and is a zoned system. Tickets can be purchased at machines in the entrance area of all stations. Most of the inner city and the attractions I describe, can be reached by an Urban ticket. You must hold your ticket since it will be needed to exit the system. When exiting the system, put your ticket in the machine and proceed through once it gives you the green light. If you are not permitted to exit because you have gone too far on the system or your time limit has expired, you will have to purchase an extra ticket and try exiting again. Remember to keep you ticket away from your cell phone so it does not de-magnetize and do not fold it as to break the magnetic strip.

Most important sights in Milan can reached by the Metropolitana. From *Centrale*, it's only ten minutes and four stops on the Yellow line to the Duomo

(Cathedral of Milan). All you need do is take the Yellow line toward S. Donato and not Comasina. Also, if you want to see Da Vinci's *Last Supper* at the *Church of Santa Maria delle Grazie*, you need to take the Metro to Cadorna, which is located on the Red and also the Green line. Remember you are in luck since you can catch the Green line from Milano *Centrale*.

DEPARTING FROM MALPENSA-MXP

It's not a big deal getting to Malpensa by train from *Milano Centrale*. However, before you set out, check your airline tickets and make sure they state you are flying out of **MXP**. If you are flying out of Linate (LIN) you will have to take a bus to the airport since there is no train service from *Centrale*. There are buses from *Centrale* to Linate airport every 30 minutes and the fare is about ten Euros.

If you are going on the *Malpensa Express* you must purchase a ticket from the ticket counter or the automated machines. The express makes the run in about 50 minutes and arrives at Terminal 1. On arrival, check your airline and if needed you can take the free shuttle bus to Terminal 2. There are about three trains per hour and the cost is about 13 Euros.

Unlike the *Leonardo Express,* the train is not a true express as it makes 6-8 stops en route. The first train, with no connections departs about 5:30 AM. This will get you into Malpensa airport about 6:30 AM in time for a minimum departure flight about 8:30 AM.

If you are terminating your rail itinerary here in Milan, and not continuing over the Alps on the *Bernina Express* to Switzerland flying home from Zurich, we do hope you enjoyed your rail journey through Italy. If you have not continued south to Naples and or Sicily, I hope that you will add these two rail journeys to your next visit to Italy.

If you are continuing your rail tour over the Alps on the *Bernina Express,* you will find it starts in the next chapter. So let's get ready to depart Milano *Centrale* for Tirano, Italy, and the *Bernina Express.*

CHAPTER 7

OVER THE ALPS ON THE *BERNINA EXPRESS*

ITINERARY C

BERNINA EXPRESS ROUGH OUT:

Day 1- Trenord train to Tirano, Italy o/n Tirano

Day 2- *Bernina Express* to Chur, o/n Chur, CH

Day 3- Swiss Rail, Chur to Zurich, o/n Zurich

Day 4- Fly back to USA from Zurich

INTRO TO THE *BERNINA EXPRESS*

If you like traveling in Europe by train, two of the most exciting trips, certainly on everyone's bucket list is to ride the *Bernina Express* over the Alps or take the *Orient Express* from Paris to Venice. Both are in the book by Patricia Schultz "*1,000 Places to See Before You Die*." The *Simplon Venice-Orient-Express* is quite costly, running about $1500 per night per person. It is truly an experience if you can afford it. However, for a fraction of the price you can experience the thrill of crossing the Alps from Italy to Switzerland on the *Bernina Express. Tripadvisor.com* rates the *Bernina Express* #5 of 893 things to do in Switzerland.

THE *GLACIER EXPRESS*

Just a note in passing, on another very popular train in the Swiss Alps known as The *Glacier Express*. It is a cousin to the *Bernina Express*. It is operated also by the Rhaetian (pronounced like radish but add the "n") Bahn Railway (RhB). However, the *Glacier Express* does not take you from Italy to Switzerland. It operates between two of the famous resort towns in the Swiss Alps, Zermatt and St. Moritz. The trip on the *Glacier Express* takes about 7.5 hours and is one of the most scenic railways in Europe. There are connections to the *Bernina Express* which will take you to Chur, Switzerland or Tirano, Italy. If you are interested in seeing the Matterhorn, one of the largest mountains in the Alps, then a side trip on the *Glacier Express* is in order. More information can be found at *glacierexpress.ch/en.*

You should note that the Rhaetian Bahn Railway is also referred as the RhB Railway and, in German, which is the primary language of most of Switzerland, is spelled *Rhatische Bahn*.

MILAN TO ZURICH IN A FLASH

If you are interested in just travelling from Milan to Zurich in a hurry, there are high speed intercity trains which make the run between the two cities in just a little over three hours using the Gotthard tunnels. It is best to consult *swissrailways.com* or *trenitalia.com*.

BRANCHES OF THE RHAETIAN RWY

Unlike the high speed intercity trains operating between Milan and Zurich, the *Bernina Express* is a tourist train; the *Bernina Express* is a train which is definitely not an express. It traverses about 90 miles in four hours, averaging about 25 miles per hour, certainly not an express in our terms. There are several branches; however, I only address one journey, which is the route from Tirano, Italy to Chur, Switzerland. The other branches of the RhB to St. Moritz and Davos, Switzerland dead-end in ski country. So if you are continuing your journey from Italy, you want to make your way to Chur and then on to Zurich, for your return flight back to the USA.

The *Bernina Express*, the all-red train with panoramic glass windows, traverses dozens of tunnels and bridges as it climbs the Alps, enters the Bernina Pass, with views of several glaciers, and descends into Chur, Switzerland. You are transported from a tropical to a frigid, almost tundra environment, and then to a temperate valley where the city of Chur is located.

A SHORT HISTORY OF THE *BERNINA EXPRESS*

Most of us Americans have probably never heard of the *Bernina Express*. So I offer you a short history of this exciting way to journey from Italy to Zurich, Switzerland for your flight home.

With the exception of several small tunnels, this train goes over the Alps from Italy to Switzerland. The rail line was completed around 1900. About thirty years prior, the Gotthard Rail Tunnel was constructed under the Alps and only in 2016 was the 33 mile Gotthard Base Tunnel opened. The Gotthard tunnels allow high speed intercity trains to operate between Milan and Zurich. It is not the *Bernina Express* route.

The area traversed and the train itself are UNESCO World Heritage sites. The train leaves daily, about 2PM (14:00), from the *Rhaetian Bahn* Railway terminal in Tirano, Italy. Other trains may be added in the summer. So, it's best to check the website *Rhb.ch.*

AN OVERVIEW OF THE ROUTE

The *Bernina Express*, named after the Bernina Pass, is one of the oddest railroads I have ever been on. Let me explain why I refer to it as "odd". It begins its journey running down one of the streets in Tirano. In about a half mile, it enters the small town of Campocologno, Switzerland. Once again, it uses a street, because the town is not wide enough to accommodate a street for automobiles and a railroad at the same time.

The train makes a short stop at Campocologno where the Swiss police (border patrol) walk the train before it departs the station. They are looking for "suspicious" characters. Now is the best time to make sure you have your passports handy if questioned. The train then exits the town, and does a loop-d-loop on what is known as the **Brusio Spiral** where you can actually see the front of the train from the rear portion of the train. I suggest you take a look at some of these pictures on the internet.

The train then climbs mountains at a 7% grade without the use of a rack and pinion (also known as a cog). What this means is that for every 100 feet the train moves forward, the track rises 7 feet. Don't be alarmed; the train is by no means a rollercoaster! You will not even notice the grade difference as the train climbs the mountains.

Special cars with oversize panoramic windows for viewing make the four hour experience delightful as the train climbs out of the tropical town of Tirano and makes its way through the small villages of the Swiss Alps. It then starts to climb the Alps, doing switchbacks several times until it reaches the summit of one mountain, enters a valley and then negotiates another mountain until it reaches the Bernina Pass. You will know you are in the Bernina Pass because you are above the tree line. Lakes appear, and off in the distance there are glaciers. Yes, even in the summer. The area is rugged and desolate. The scenery is breathtaking!

From the pass, the train will slowly descend (in elevation) below the tree line as it crosses back and forth over the Abula River as it works its way down from the mountains and into the historic city of Chur (pronounced core).

In summary, over a four hour period you go from Tirano, Italy which has a Mediterranean tropical climate with palm trees to the snow-covered Alps and the remaining glaciers of Europe and then back to a valley of Switzerland with a moderate climate, all with breathtaking views.

COST OF THE *BERNINA EXPRESS*

What's surprising about the *Bernina Express* from Tirano to Chur is the cost. First class tickets cost about 125 Euros and second class tickets about 75 Euros. Seating is either two across from each other or four on a table. All coaches have ultra-modern toilet facilities. Best is to book your seats directly on the RhB website, *Rhb.ch*. Reservations usually open up ninety days before the day of departure.

If you are using one of the rail passes i.e. Eurail, Swiss Rail or any other, you will find that the *Bernina*

Express honors all, except the Eurail Italy Rail pass. In addition if you are using a valid rail pass you must still reserve a seat and pay the reservation fee, which you can do on line.

CAUTION: DON'T DO IT IN A DAY

Even though the journey from Milan to Chur and on to Zurich could be done in one calendar day, my recommendation is to follow my itinerary below and the rough out above. I don't know about you, but eight to eleven hours on three trains in one day with your bags in two is just too much for me and does take away from the experience. So here is how to plan your over the Alps experience for maximum enjoyment.

Remember, you want to go on the *Bernina Express* from Tirano to Chur. It operates once a day. However, check schedules with the website *Rhb.ch*. You do not want to go to St. Moritz or Davos, unless you intend to ski or overnight there before coming back down the mountain and catching the *Bernina Express* again to Chur. You need not go back to Tirano as there are connections to the Chur line. Now here is my suggested itinerary.

>>>TIP<<<

Before we get going, here is another suggestion. When you pack your bags the evening before in Milan, do pack your jacket and a sweater on the top (of the inside) of your bag. It does get sometimes chilly in the evening in Tirano and Chur, yes, even in the summer! Okay, so here is the itinerary.

>>>>><<<<<

DAY 1- MILANO *CENTRALE* TO TIRANO, ITALY

The jumping off stop for the *Bernina Express* is Tirano, Italy. However, you first have to make your way to Tirano which is a moderate size town located on the Italian-Swiss border at the base of the Italian-Swiss Alps, about 100 miles northeast of Milan. Tirano is the end of the line. So don't worry, you won't miss your station.

The Trenord Regional train makes the journey from Milano *Centrale* every one to two hours. If you followed my day trip to Lake Como and took the train to Varenna-Esino, it will be the same train. The running time is about 2.5 hours and the cost usually runs about 11.50 Euros per person one way. You should consider buying your tickets when you arrive in *Centrale* from Venice or else you can do it the day before. Also, do ask for the senior discount. If you are using a rail pass it may be best to just pay the cash fee instead of using up a day of travel for such a small amount of money. You will certainly need your rail pass on the journey from Tirano, Italy to Chur, Switzerland on the *Bernina Express* if you are using a Eurail pass, (not an Italy Eurail pass).

There are two time frames to arrive in Tirano. If you are all shopped-out or sight-seed out in Milan, then it's best to take a morning train to Tirano to arrive about noon or 1 PM (13:00). If your hotel room is not available, the hotel will allow you to check your bags in the baggage room or they will watch your bags. You can then go to lunch or shop in this lovely town.

The alternate approach is to leave Milan in the early afternoon, say about 1 PM (13:00) and arrive in Tirano about 4 PM (16:00). However, this will not allow you lots of time to see the town or shop. You will have to reserve this for tomorrow after breakfast. It's your choice. Now, here is a short description of this lovely town nestled against the Alps.

Picture this: Abutting a rather large cobble stone square, there are several European style hotels and Bed & Breakfasts. Don't expect a Holiday Inn or a Marriott, you won't find one! The plaza or square is home to about a dozen restaurants, cafes, and gelato shops. One or two blocks from the square, you will find lots of shops, everything from supermarkets to clothing stores. If you want to do your laundry you will find the "Lavapiu" laundromat about five blocks from the square.

Now here is the oddest thing. There are two rail stations in the same square; yes, two! The Trenitalia (Trenord) long green trains arrive at one station and the *Bernina Express* bright red trains depart from another station across the square which serves the Rhaetian Bahn Railway (RhB). You should note that RhB trains also depart for St. Moritz and other points in the Swiss Alps from the RhB station.

After departing *Centrale* (with your snacks and drinks) you will arrive in Tirano in 2.5 hours. If you did not get a chance to view Lake Como, it's best that you grab a seat on the left-hand side for some good views.

In about ninety minutes after passing Varenna-Esino you will arrive at the end of the line in Tirano. You exit the Trenord Regional train station with your bags and go directly across the square to your hotel. It should be less than a three minute walk. It's best to make this reservation several months before you leave the USA since many of the hotels on the square fill up fast. There are lots of other hotels in the town; however, you may have to take a short taxi ride. This should not cost you more than ten Euros.

Our favorite hotel is the Hotel Bernina. It is a three star hotel with an elevator, serves an excellent buffet breakfast (included) and has a superb restaurant. I would suggest you make a dinner reservation on arrival at your hotel. If you would like to stay at the Hotel Bernina, book direct at *booking@saintjane.it* which is their parent company. Make sure you state Hotel Bernina as they have other hotels in Italy. There are other hotels and nice B&Bs on the square and a few blocks away. Best to check their location with the *Booking.com* map feature.

So check into your hotel. Enjoy lunch, and a gelato, do some shopping, (last chance for Italian souvenirs) take a snooze, have dinner and get ready for tomorrow. One more item; all those other people you see in the square, the restaurants and hotels will also be on the RhB railway tomorrow bound for Switzerland.

DAY 2- *BERNINA EXPRESS* TO CHUR

Have breakfast and check your bags at the front desk or in the baggage room. If you are on the afternoon train, which usually departs about 2 PM (14:00) you will have ample time to shop and have lunch in the square. Also, pickup some snacks at one of the grocery stores located about two blocks off the square with other shops, on the *Viale Italia*.

About thirty minutes before your departure on the *Bernina Express*, retrieve your bags at the hotel and head for the Rhaetian Bahn Railway station. Have the ticket window people check your tickets and advise you of the proper track. Once again, note that those red trains also go to different locations like St. Moritz, so make sure you board the *Bernina Express*. Also, if you want to take pictures of the train, now is the time, since you probably will be in a rush to get to your hotel after arriving in Chur.

Once the track is announced, find your car, board the train and locate your seats. After stowing your bags make sure you have all your personal belongings. You are now ready to go over the Alps.

I won't describe all details of the trip as they are described on many websites. Best to just Google *Bernina Express*, and do look at all those pictures.

Don't worry about which side of the train has the best view. You will see people taking pictures from each side. Since there are lots of switchbacks it really doesn't matter, as you will have the other view in a few minutes when the train reverses direction. All the seats afford an excellent view of the territory traversed.

>>>TIP<<<

There is a lot of glare from the panoramic window's reflections. You can take better pictures from the drop down windows located next to the toilets. Importantly, hold your cameras or smart-phones tightly; avoid holding them outside the window. If dropped out of the window by accident, I can assure you the train will NOT stop to assist you in retrieving it. In addition, it's best to avoid taking selfies by hanging the selfie-stick outside of the window.

>>>>><<<<<

Enjoy the breathtaking views. In about four hours you will arrive in Chur.

When planning your trip and making your hotel reservations, remember that things will cost more in Switzerland, and especially in Chur and Zurich. You should figure everything is about double than what you would expect to pay in Italy. The hotels follow the same rules. A three star hotel will cost you almost $200, instead of about $100.

On arrival in Chur, you can walk to your hotel or take a taxi for about seven Swiss francs. At the time of this writing the Swiss franc was worth about one dollar. Most of the hotels in this town are less than ten francs away from the rail station. There are several hotels around the train station; consult Chapter 11 for info.

When you exit the train, you will go down below the tracks to an underground passage. The question is do you exit to your right or to your left. Best is to exit to your right as you come down the stairs since there are more taxis on this side of the rail station, but it's no big deal if you exit to the left.

It is smart to observe this station, since you will return tomorrow to catch your train to Zurich. Take note of where you purchase your Swiss Rail tickets. Also, note that they will not depart on the same track you arrived on since the *Bernina Express* uses a different track gauge than the high speed Swiss Rail trains.

Also, it's best to stay in the old historic district of Chur with its narrow streets, shops and restaurants. This town actually dates back to 3900 BC and is, in fact, the oldest town in Switzerland. Our favorite lodging is the Ambiente Hotel Freieck (*Freieck.ch*). The Freieck offers great views of the old city (ask for a room with a nice view of the city). The rooms are excellent and the breakfast more than bountiful.

If time permits, take in some shopping in the old city and stroll the "*Poststrasse*" or consider a snooze before dinner. It's best to do all your final shopping here, as you may not have time in the big city of Zurich, unless you will be shopping for bars of gold bullion.

For dinner there are several excellent restaurants within a three block walk of the Freieck hotel and the other hotels in the area. Our favorite is the *Ticino Restaurante*, about a block away from the Freieck. Within a few blocks you will also find lots of pubs with excellent food.

DAY 3- CHUR TO ZURICH

After that bountiful breakfast, consider shopping in the Chur's old city if you have not done so. The front desk at your hotel will be glad to watch your bags while you do your shopping. After a light lunch, make your way back to the hotel to pick up your bags and head for the station for the 60-90 minute train ride to Zurich. Do check the evening before with the receptionist for the schedule for the Zurich bound trains. Swiss Rail offers trains which make limited stops and take about one hour. The local trains take about 90 minutes, and yes, Swiss Rail will gladly take all types of credit cards. There is a train every hour to Zurich HB (*Hauptbahnhof*) station and you need not make reservations. First class as well as second class is offered. And, as usual make sure you mind your bags. Seat reservations are most of the time not possible and in addition, unlike Italy with a 120 day window, you can only book 30 days ahead in Switzerland. By the way, the price is about 18-36 Euros per person depending on time of day. So check with Swiss Rail on line before you leave the USA, however, my recommendation is to purchase your tickets at the rail station in Chur after you arrive on the *Bernina Express.*

About 30 minutes prior to your train's departure to Zurich, you should make your way with your bags to Chur's central train station. Yes the one you arrived at yesterday on the *Bernina Express*. If it's not walking distance, do have the receptionist at your hotel call a taxi. On arrival at the train station, purchase your tickets (ask for any senior discounts or present your Eurail Pass) and head for the track where the train will depart. Board your train and do make sure it is bound for Zurich HB.

On arrival at Zurich HB station, bear to the right where you will find taxis or walk a few blocks to your hotel. You should ask the taxi driver what the cost would be approximately in Euros to your hotel. Remember, in Switzerland, everything is about double the price of elsewhere. If you will be in Switzerland only a few days, you will find that they will take your Euros except they will not take any coins. They will also by law give you back your change in Swiss francs. So best just to use your credit cards where possible instead of obtaining Swiss francs from an ATM. I should note that most taxis do take credit cards. Technically the only item you will need Swiss francs for is tips and café items, which can be paid in Euros.

DAY 4- FLY HOME FROM ZURICH

You should allow a minimum of four hours from the time you leave your hotel to your actual departure time back to the USA.

There is no need to worry about catching a train to the Zurich airport (ZHR) today. Trains depart Zurich HB every 10 minutes for the airport. The fare is about seven Euros and takes about 10-15 minutes. Also, if you prefer not to take the train, the fixed fare via a taxi to Zurich airport is about $65-$70. Yikes! But don't worry, they all take credit cards. Another idea I often recommend is to change trains at Zurich HB when you arrive from Chur, and head directly to the airport via the train the evening before your flight home instead of staying in the city. When you arrive at the airport, you can usually be transferred to your airport area hotel via a courtesy van. Contact your hotel via email for this service when making your booking and before you leave the USA. Also, consider location and services at the hotel you will be booking. Some hotels do not have any restaurant and may be far away from any. Do enquire directly with the hotel.

Enjoy your flight back to the USA.

We do hope you enjoyed this book and look forward to seeing you on the trains of Spain (RENFE) sometime in 2020 in my new book SPAIN—*The Best Places to See by Rail.*

CHAPTER 8

THE AMALFI EXTENSION

ITINERARY D

THE AMALFI ROUGH OUT:
Day 1- Depart Rome for Naples and our base
      in Sorrento (4 nights) or fly to NAP
Day 2- The *Circumvesuviana* train to the ruins of
      Pompeii and Herculaneum
Day 3- A day on the Amalfi Coast- The Amalfi Drive
Day 4- A day on the Island of Capri
Day 5- Depart Naples for Florence or Rome

INTRODUCTION
I refer to this chapter as the Amalfi Extension as most people know this region as Amalfi. However, it is actually a section of the region known as Campania. On this rail tour I highlight the three main attractions: Sorrento, the Amalfi coast and the island of Capri. Sorrento and other towns comprise what is known as the Sorrentine Peninsula. Likewise, the Amalfi coast

165

is comprised of such towns as Positanto, Ravello, Amalfi, and Praiano and many other smaller towns.

For those of you who have another five days available in Italy, you can start your rail trip in Rome and then continue on south to the Naples area, before going on the Three Capitals Tour (Itinerary A). Yes, it does require you to go south to Naples and then back north. However, this is not a problem on your return to the north, as you do not have to go through Rome to get to Florence or Venice, since the high speed trains bypass Rome.

You can also start your trip by flying into Naples. Most of the European airlines including Lufthansa, Alitalia, and Air France have flights from their hubs directly to Naples. So if you are flying in from, say, Chicago on Swiss Air, you can fly to Zurich and connect with a Swiss Air flight to Naples. You then follow this itinerary and then take the train to Rome and begin your Itinerary A. You can also do Rome as part of Itinerary A, then go to Naples and then on to Florence.

>>>TIP<<<

If you are starting your trip in Naples, remember you are best to add a recovery day at your hotel in

Sorrento, since you will be entirely wiped out from your overnight flight from the USA.

On the return trip to the north, Trenitalia and Italo have express trains which leave Naples every two hours for Florence (and every hour for Rome), so it's not a big deal. The high speed TGV type trains make the sprint in about three hours to Florence (Rome in a little over an hour) at a cost of about thirty Euros.

So first let's get down to the Naples area: Naples, Pompeii, Sorrento, The island of Capri and the Amalfi Coast.

DAY 1- NAPLES VIA THE *ITALO*

After several days in Rome, pack your bags and head down to Roma *Termini.* If you are at one of the hotels abutting *Termini,* it's easy. If not, you can certainly take a taxi for 10-15 Euros. Best is to get a train about 10 AM. This will get you to your hotel in Sorrento about 1 PM (13:00) with enough time for a snooze or shopping. The competing high speed trains operated by Italo make the journey in one hour and ten minutes (same time as Trenitalia) at a cost of 15-20 Euros if

167

you get the right train, hardly worth the use of a five day Eurail Pass (which cannot be used on Italo). I should say Italo tries to compete with the "quasi" government owned Trenitalia. However, since you will be travelling Trenitalia (or Trenord) through most of Italy, now is the best time to try the competition with their sleek burgundy trains designed by the president of Ferrari and manufactured by Alstom. These people at Alstom haven't missed anything. You name it, wifi, leather seats, A/C receptacles, are all there with plenty of comfort and room for the bags.

WHY STAY IN SORRENTO?

Many people ask me all the time— "Why not Positano or Naples?" It's simple. Positano is rather hilly; steep would be a better word. It is not accessible by rail and most parts are not accessible even by car. If you stay here you will need a lot of energy to lug your bags up several flights of cobblestone steps. Those little blue mini buses from Sorrento described below only navigate the main drive. However, Sorrento is the best jumping off spot for attractions in and around the Sorrentine Peninsular and the Amalfi Coast. So if you want to go to Capri for the day, take the Amalfi Drive to Amalfi, do some great shopping, stay at a stately hotel, then Sorrento is the place. What's better is that it's flat. Yup, no walking up lots of steps and, of course, it is served by rail.

Now, about Naples; nothing really to say. However, you can check it out on your own. Read the article "Why no one wants to travel to Naples" from *businessinsider.com*. Frankly, I would rather spend a weekend in Hoboken, New Jersey, where I can still enjoy a great slice of pizza at Grimaldi's without having to worry about being pick-pocked. However, don't sell Naples short. It is, of course, the railhead for all those trains from the north and the hub of the area. It has some fine museums and great cemeteries. That's right, even Enrico Caruso the famous opera singer is buried here. However, the real attractions of the area lie outside of Naples. Enough said!

THE CIRCUMVESUVIANA RAILWAY

Once you arrive in Naples *Centrale,* follow the signs to the *Circumvesuviana.* This commuter train goes to the Sorrentine Peninsula and other towns. It is named for the dormant (hopefully for now) volcano Vesuvius. You should also make sure the train is bound for Sorrento since there are several other destinations.

You do not need a reservation and there is a train every 20 minutes. It's like a New York City subway. You pay for your ticket about four Euros, and get off at the last stop Sorrento— end of the line. Note the trains are not air-conditioned and have no place for your baggage. So place your bags on the seat next to you, if available, and keep an eye on them. Also, note the train does not go down the famous Amalfi Drive, but we will tell you how you can.

>>>>TIP<<<

There are also 4-6 express trains a day operating on the *Circumvesuviana* Railway which make only four stops on their way to Sorrento (instead of two dozen). The trains are called the *Campania Express*, and the cost is about eight Euros. Sometimes, they only run in the high season. The trains are air-conditioned. Bear in mind that you cannot use your rail passes on any trains of the *Circumvesuviana* Railway. For more info consult *eavsrl.it*.

>>>>><<<<<

OH SORRENTO, SORRENTO

On arrival in Sorrento, you can either walk to your hotel or take a taxi. Sorrento is not that big. There is shopping in town and you can catch the high speed boat (hydrofoil) for a day trip to the island of Capri. If you want to experience the famous Amalfi Drive you can either hire a driver to take you to Amalfi or take one of those blue mini-buses outside the Sorrento stazione. There will be more on this later.

>>>TIP<<<

If you are looking for a nice centrally located hotel, my recommendation is always the Hotel Antiche Mura. It is only a five minute walk to the *Piazza Tasso* and the shopping on the *Corso Italia*. However, do watch the rates as they change dramatically by season of the year. Many other hotels are right in town. If you want a view of the Bay of Naples you will pay extra!

>>>>><<<<<

DAY 2- NAPLES AND POMPEII

Consider visiting Pompeii via the Circumvesuviana in the morning. Pompeii is an entire city that was discovered in 1848. It was entirely buried when Mount Vesuvius erupted in the year AD 79. The train makes the journey from Sorrento to Pompeii in about 45 minutes. The entrance is about 200 feet from the exit of the station. Entrance fee runs about 20 Euros per person. Once again ask for the senior discount if available. You should consider spending about two hours here. The size of the place is mind boggling. Do visit both amphitheatres and the house of ill repute. After you are finished with Pompeii you will probably be bushed. So my suggestion would be to return to Sorrento for a snooze before dinner. If you have a lot of energy still left, get back on the Circumvesuviana and go to Naples for a few hours, where you will find lots of good museums or visit Herculaneum which is another historic site only minutes away.

If you have a lot of energy still left from all that walking at the ruins of Pompeii, my suggestion would be to visit the ruins of Herculaneum which is another UNESCO World Heritage site. It is located in the small village of Ercolano where you can also enjoy lunch with the locals. To reach the site, all you need do is get back on the Circumvesuviana bound for Naples and get off in about 15 minutes at *Ercolano Scavi.* Note that there are two stops with the name *Ercolano.* Scavi means ruins— think scavenger hunt. After exiting the train station it's only a ten minute walk all downhill.

When returning to Sorrento, make sure you get a train bound for Sorrento as *Ercolano Scavi* is served by trains bound for other destinations in the Vesuvius area.

DAY 3- THE AMALFI DRIVE

The Amalfi Drive is one of those things you must experience and the best way to do it is with a private driver for a half day or an entire day (*sorrentocars.com also known as Leonardotravels.com*). A private driver for the day will cost you $200-$300. If you have another couple to join you this might be the best approach. *Leonardo Travels* also has a six passenger min-van. A private tour with a few stops is the best way to visit the towns of the Amalfi Coast.

The next best alternative only for $12 a person, is to go down (and back up) the Amalfi Drive at your leisure via the SITA vans. Those little blue vans operated by SITA leave the Sorrento *Circumvesuviana* train station about every 45 minutes. My suggestion would be to take the van either to Positano or Amalfi and have lunch, then return to Sorrento in the afternoon. You need to purchase your tickets at any tobacco, bar or magazine stand at the train station. The van driver does not sell tickets!

Consider also an all day ticket for eight Euros which allows you to get on and off the van at all the towns. It is good for eight hours of travel. Also, remember to frank or validate your ticket in the yellow machine when entering the van for the first time. Also take note that there are no toilets on the van.

If you do not get off the van at Positano, Praiano, Ravello or any intermediate stops it will take you 1.45 hours to make the trip from Sorrento to Amalfi. Amalfi is also a good place to have lunch. Unlike Positano and Praiano it has a large "flat" area abutting the sea. Here you will find convenient cafes and restaurants in and around *Piazza Flavio Gioia* which is one of the main squares.

>>>TIP<<<

You need to be on the right hand side of the van on the way down the Drive and on the left hand side on the return. Note suggest you be at the van loading spot about 20 minutes before departure; else you will not get a good seat and may even stand!

>>>>><<<<<

>>>TIP<<<

For you seniors, if you need to take a break, use the facilities or grab a café, consider buying that all day ticket and getting off at each town when needed. Here are the most popular towns and transit times between them in transit order:

Sorrento to Positano 40 minutes;

Positano to Praiano 30 minutes;

Praiano to Conca dei Marini 30 minutes;

Conca dei Marini to Amalfi 20 minutes;

If you have to ask "How many minutes to xxxx", use the phrase *"Quanti minuti a xxxx"*.

>>>>><<<<<

For a change in scenery, consider taking the high speed hydrofoil back to Sorrento from Positano. It's less than $25 per person and makes the trip back in about an hour. Consult *naplesbayferry.com*. The Amalfi Drive makes California's Pacific Coast Highway look like a straight line! No tour buses are allowed on the Amalfi Drive because of the curves.

A worthwhile stop for about 40 minutes is the *Villa Rufolo* at Ravello. It is best to consult the SITA blue van schedule at *ravello.com/sita-bus-schedule*. This is a gorgeous villa with magnificent gardens overlooking the sea. If you care to have lunch instead of a visit to *Rufolo*, consider the Hotel Villa Cimbrone, also in Ravello. This villa was converted to a hotel in the mid 1990's. Note, Ravello is a few miles past Amalfi going toward Salerno. If you happen to make it to Salerno, you can take the train back to Naples and then get the Circumvesuviana back to Sorrento. Make sure you board the Sorrento train!

DAY 4- A DAY ON CAPRI

It's "Cap-ree" not "Kahpree"! So let's make sure you pronounce it correctly. All you need remember is CAP; yes, just like a baseball cap on your head. Capri is an island in the Bay of Naples easily reachable by hydrofoils and ferries from Sorrento and Naples in about forty minutes. It is about the size of Manhattan's Central Park. It is one big piece of sandstone and lime-rock and was inhabited about 2,000 years ago by the Ancient Romans. Now it's a be seen place for the rich and famous. If you don't own a home on Lake Como, then you have a villa on Capri.

Capri is one of those adult Disneylands like Monte Carlo. It's in a world of its own, certainly worth a day trip just to say "I was there." Picture this: Very chic five star hotels surrounded by high-end designer shops e.g. Gucci, Dior, and Bulgari. If you don't see classy models and Hollywood personalities darting around, you will see the paparazzi chasing them. They wait outside shops and hotels like lions hovering in a pack waiting for their prey. As soon as they see their target, they go in for the kill and shoot hundreds of pictures in less than five seconds. They are all over the place. But Capri has more to offer than just watching those paparazzi photographers.

GETTING TO CAPRI

From Sorrento, it's best to take the hi-speed hydrofoil for the day to Capri. I suggest this to my friends instead of going back to Naples on the Circumvesuviana and then hiking over to the ferry terminal. In season, there are also ferries from Amalfi, Positano and Salerno. The trip on the high speed hydrofoil from Sorrento makes the journey to the island in a little less than thirty minutes (almost one hour from Naples). The hydrofoil does not take automobiles. The round-trip cost is about forty Euros, and they do take credit cards. The hydrofoil leaves Sorrento from the Marina Piccolo about every 40 minutes.

>>>TIP<<<

You might want to consider the day trip to Capri as the first full day in Sorrento. If the sea is rough, they usually cancel the hydrofoils. So if you arrive at the ferry terminal and there is a notice **"NO FERRIES TODAY TO CAPRI,"** you can plan on going to Pompeii or taking the Amalfi Drive.

>>>>><<<<<

It is a short walk down hill to the Marina Piccolo where the hydrofoil departs. This is less than a quarter mile from the *Piazza Tasso* the main square of Sorrento. You can walk it easily in 15 minutes. On the return, it's a different story. It's a steep hill up to the *Piazza Tasso* and my suggestion would be to take a taxi from the Marina Piccolo to your hotel. Trust me, you will be bushed! Taxis meet the arriving hydrofoils, so you won't be stranded at the pier.

Allow plenty of time before the hydrofoil departs to buy your round trip tickets and do note the return schedule if you don't want to spend the night on a park bench or a beach on Capri.

>>>TIP<<<

On boarding the hydrofoil, you want to sit on the left side (port) since there are breathtaking views of the Sorrento landscape. If you sit on the right (starboard) all you will see is water.

>>>>><<<<<

You should target getting a hydrofoil 10-11 AM. This will allow you to have a late lunch on the island and view the highlights. There is a snack bar and facilities on the hydrofoil. It would be best to return on a 5 PM (17:00) or 6 PM (18:00) hydrofoil back to Sorrento. Do enjoy a cold beer or a glass of wine on your return.

It's best to ask your hotel concierge or front desk person about the hydrofoil schedules a day or two before your planned visit. Also, a taxi to the Marina Piccolo will cost 5-10 Euros from the hotels suggested.

WHAT TO DO IN CAPRI?

First you have to know that there are two Capris. One is called Capri and the other is on top of the island and is called *Anacapri*. Unless you want to take a full island tour, best is to just visit Capri. This is where all the hotels, restaurants and shops are located. Anacapri has more of the mansions, villas and big homes.

THE BLUE GROTTO

Before reading this section you might want to visit the reviews on *tripadvisor.com* pertaining to the Blue Grotto of Capri. On arrival at the ferry terminal (Marina Grande), there will be several dozen hawkers trying to convince you to take their boat to The Blue Grotto. It's about a two hour tour on a small boat. And, I do mean a small boat. Yup, it probably will not have a toilet and the sea may get rough on your way down the island. So, best not to attempt this after lunch!

The Blue Grotto is a sea cave where the blue light from the water is reflected upwards onto the ceiling of the cave. If it's a nice day, the sea is calm, and you are there about the noon hour, you might consider taking the tour. For a group of people, you can usually negotiate the price. Also, the small boat you will be on does not actually go into the cave. It's about a 15 minute ride to the grotto. Once there, you must transfer to a smaller boat the size of a canoe, since the entrance to the cave is roughly five feet wide. Many times during the day there is a queue for those canoes once you arrive up island from the ferry terminal. This can take upwards of one hour! You will only be in the sea cave about two minutes. Also, note that many of these grotto guys are ex-fishermen (or they fish in morning) and they do not take credit cards.

On arrival at the Marina Grande, if you are going to the Blue Grotto or going to take an island tour, you do not take the funicular up to the square. Here are my suggestions for the balance of the day on Capri:

If you want to take a one hour tour of the island including Capri and *Anacapri* (recommended), do negotiate with one of the taxi drivers at the Marina Grande to take you on a tour. Depending on the number of taxis and the time of the year, prices may vary. A good thing to do is split the one hour cost with another couple. Also, you should note that taxis are pretty much off limits to the area around the main square of Capri town. You will see many golf carts delivering everything from cases of beer to personal luggage. So best is to leave this area around the square for your after-lunch stroll.

To make it easy on all, there is a *funivia* which will take you to the top of Capri (not *Anacapri*) where the main square is located. I recommend a one way ticket since you can take a nice stroll down to the ferry terminal for your return trip to Sorrento instead of taking the *funivia*. Along this stroll there are lots of shops where you can buy inexpensive jewelry and food. The stroll without shopping takes about 15 minutes from the square to the Marina Grande.

The funicular (*funivia*) will whisk you to the *Piazza Umberto I square*, which is the main square of Capri town in about four minutes. It cost fewer than two dollars—what a bargain. Once in the main square you can visit the church, stroll the main walkways, shop and view the paparazzi darting around, trying to snap pictures of Sophia Loren, Kate Upton or Mariah Carey. It's a lot of fun to just sit on one of those benches outside of a hotel and just people-watch, and of course enjoy your gelato.

After your lunch and shopping, head on down to the Marina Grande ferry terminal to catch your return hydrofoil back to the Marina Piccolo in Sorrento, about 5 PM (17:00). You probably will be too bushed to walk up that big hill to the *Piazza Tasso*, so just take a taxi to take you to your hotel.

>>>TIP<<<

There is an excellent restaurant in Sorrento with popular prices. In fact, it's so good that on my last trip I even went there twice. The name of it is *Da Filippo* and the best thing about it is that they will pick you up at your hotel and after dinner they will deliver you back to your hotel—at no charge! All you need do is have your concierge or the front desk manager at your hotel give them a call, make a reservation and they will pick you up. This is the place the locals go to and the seafood and fish are great, not to mention the décor.

>>>>><<<<<

This concludes the Amalfi extension.

If you are going now to Rome to begin your Three Capitals Tour, make sure you buy your tickets on Trenitalia or Italo for the high speed morning train back to Rome. Remember, you must allow 2.5 hours minimum to get to Napoli *Centrale*, and then take your bags to the main station located above the Circumvesuviana. You will need this available time to purchase some food at the station for your journey as food on the trains is quite costly. I might note there are porters available who will lug your bags on the cart for a few Euros. So if you have a 10:00 AM train to

Rome, Florence, or Sicily plan on getting to the *Circumvesuviana* station at Sorrento about 7:30 AM.

If you are not travelling by rail and are heading to the Naples airport for your return flight to the USA, you will find that the Alibus (*anm.it/*) operates several times an hour to whisk you to Naples airport in about 15 minutes for only five Euros. There is no rail service to the airport from Naples *Centrale*.

I hope you enjoyed your visit to the Amalfi and Sorrentine area and hopefully you will continue north on the Three Capitals Tour or go south to Sicily, which follows this chapter.

CHAPTER 9

THE SICILY EXTENSIONS

ITINERARY E

SICILY INTRODUCTION

Sicily, not to be confused with the other large island of Sardinia, is the big island the toe of the Italian boot is kicking. Many of the temples and ruins found on the island predate the Roman and Greek empires. In fact, no one even knows who built the Temple of Segesta which is located a few kilometers from Trapani, on the northwest corner of the island. The other historic ruins which you may consider visiting are Segesta, the Valley of the Temples at Agrigento (absolutely mind boggling) and the temple at Selinunte. All of these three archeological sites can be visited on a day trip from your base in Trapani/Erice or Palermo. Also to be considered is the ancient city of Syracuse, which dates to Greek and Roman times.

185

If you are into real history, Sicily is the place. However Sicily has a major problem, mostly created by nature. There are mountains and lots of mountains, including Mount Etna which is a semi-active or dormant for now volcano. It is located in the northeast corner. Etna erupts every couple of years, not a big deal! These mountains coupled with man-made problems create difficult rail travel within Sicily, for several reasons.

SICILY RAIL SERVICE EXPLAINED

It would not be fair to exclude a rail extension to Sicily. Sicily is part of Italy even though the people think of themselves first as Sicilians. In fact, many speak Sicilian. Visiting Sicily by rail is quite easy to do but extremely challenging. While getting to Palermo or Catania, two major cities of Sicily, from Naples or Rome is quite easy to do, the rest of Sicily is difficult or nearly impossible to reach by rail.

Travelling by train within Sicily defines the words *"You can't get there from here."* The island is very mountainous. With the exception of the *Bernina Express*, trains usually don't climb up mountains. Add to this, the rail system is mostly single track and the towns are spread out. And get this—I think they have the slowest trains in all of Italy. In fact, most of the towns have absolutely no rail service. And whatever you do, don't ask someone at a hotel in Palmero how to get to Trapani by train. They will laugh at you and think it's a joke!

Last year I drove my car from Palermo to Trapani, a distance of 65 miles. It took me 90 minutes with a quick rest stop. To go by train you must take a bus and a train. It's a four hour journey and will eat up your whole day. Certainly not worth the time you will spend on a train and a bus. Here's another example of the problem: To go from Agrigento to Syracuse will take you almost six hours with two transfers. Yikes!

There has got to be a better way, and there is. I have developed two itineraries to see the highlights of Sicily. One is called Sicily-West and the other is Sicily-East. I will explain them later but first let's get down to Palermo, the capital city of Sicily and our jumping off spot for the Sicily-West itinerary. If you are only going to do the Sicily-East itinerary and start in Taormina, you still need to take the same train down the Italian mainland from either Rome or Naples.

NAPLES/ROME TO PALERMO
HOW IT WORKS

Your best approach is to continue your itinerary from Naples after doing the Amalfi Extension (Chapter 8). After departing Naples on one of the high-speed intercity trains, you will arrive at *Villa San Giovanni* on the Straits of Messina in about 3.5-4 hours. Here the high-speed train is placed on a ferry for the water crossing. Now, here is the key; one end of the train will go west to Palermo and the other will go south to Taormina and Catania, ultimately on to Syracuse (Siracusa). So you must make sure you are on the right car, or you will go south to Catania instead of going west to Palermo! You should not panic as the train actually divides at Messina *Centrale* about 15 minutes after it arrives at the port.

If you are going to Palermo, which I suggest, the travel time from Napoli *Centrale* will be about 9.5 hours at a cost of about thirty Euros. You can also take a night train for twenty Euros more. In this way, you will not have to pay for a hotel room in Palermo, once you arrive in the morning. However, I do not advise this as it's like flying to Europe overnight. You will probably arrive bushed, as it is difficult to sleep on a train. So the best option is to take the morning train which departs about 10 AM and arrives in Palermo about 7 PM (19:00), just in time for dinner! A train about 2 PM (14:00) arrives about 11 PM (23:00). However, you will have to skip that great Sicilian dinner and settle for a Panini if you can find a place open at that hour to get one. Best to be prepared before you leave Naples.

Now, if you are going to start your Sicilian rail tour using the Sicily-East itinerary, your running time from Naples to Catania will be 7-8 hours. However, consider getting off the train at Taormina since the station comes up about 45 minutes before Catania (the big city on the east coast). I have been to Catania and my feeling is that it is just another big city. You should also remember to wake up if you are taking a night train. Once again, this is not advisable. If you get the 10 AM train from Naples, you will get into Taormina about 5 PM (17:00), perfect time for checking into your hotel and having dinner. However, it is best to start your Sicily journey at Palermo if you are doing the Sicily-West itinerary first.

After you finish the Sicily-West itinerary you have two choices: You can continue with the Sicily-East itinerary or go back to Palermo and fly back to the USA from there, or take the train back to Naples or

Rome. If you are going to do the Sicily-East itinerary after the Sicily-West itinerary, you still need to go back to Palermo. If you are flying out of Catania (CTA) you will also need to go back to Palermo and take the train to Catania (via Messina *Centrale*). Once again, this is a place where you cannot get there from here.

Now, finally, if you are only doing the Sicily-East itinerary (coming from Rome or Naples) and visiting Taormina, Mt. Etna and Siracusa, you need to follow the Sicily-East itinerary and once again, definitely make sure you are on the right car when that train leaves Messina *Centrale.* If you are coming over from Palermo you will have to change trains in Messina *Centrale.*

If you are originating your Sicily journey from Rome, all you need do is add 2 hours on to my times stated above. That same train going to Sicily and stopping at Naples originated at Rome *Termini* two hours earlier. Once the train arrives in Naples, Trenitalia needs time to change crews, provision the train and then load the passengers. When that's done the train departs for the high speed run to Sicily.

SUMMARY OF SICILY WEST & EAST

You can do the West or the East only, or both. Here are the highlights of both:

HIGHLIGHTS SICILY-WEST:

Palermo and its Cathedral (3 street markets)
Trapani Shopping (3 street markets)
The hilltop medieval town of Erice
The temple at Segesta
The temple at Selinunte
The Valley of the Temples at Agrigento

HIGHLIGHTS SICILY-EAST:

The hilltop medieval town of Taormina
A rail trip around Mt. Etna volcano
    via the Circumetnea Railway
Syracuse (Siracusa) with its Greek and Roman ruins

SICILY-WEST ROUGH-OUT:

Day 1 - Trenitalia Train from Naples or Rome
      to Palermo (o/n Palermo)
Day 2- Palermo the Cathedral and the old city
      (o/n Palermo)
Day 3- Day trip to Agrigento (o/n Palermo)
Day 4- Bus from Palermo to Trapani
      (o/n Trapani or Erice)

Day 5- Day trip to the temple at Segesta
          (o/n Trapani or Erice)
Day 6- Day trip to the temple at Selinunte
          (o/n Trapani or Erice)
Day 7- Bus back to Palermo and fly back to USA
             -or-

          Continue via train to Taormina
          starting the Sicily-East itinerary
o/n= Overnight

DAY 1 - NAPLES OR ROME TO PALERMO

We start our Sicily-West tour via rail from either Rome or Naples. Note again, anything other than the train about 10 AM from Naples (or 8 AM from Rome) will be a hassle i.e. difficult finding your hotel at night, and missing an excellent Sicilian dinner. So it is best to take my advice. We arrive in Palermo 5-7 PM and check into our hotel.

>>>TIP<<<

While the journey is long, you probably will be on an ETR high-speed intercity train with all those conveniences including pricey food. So it is best to buy your sandwiches, snacks and drinks at the stazione before boarding the train. Make sure you leave enough time at *Termini* or Naples *Centrale*. As a seasoned traveler I can tell you that leaving enough time and arriving early relieves all that stress.

>>>>><<<<<

You will find all the information on finding and boarding your train to Sicily in Chapter 5, The Three Capitals tour.

>>>TIP<<<

Depending on the season, you will find the sun setting on the right hand side of the train. So if you enjoy sunsets, best to sit on the right side.

>>>>><<<<<

On arrival at Palermo *Centrale*, you should have lots of energy if you were sitting on the train all day. By the way, as in travelling to Europe overnight, it's a good idea to "walk the train" several times during your journey to get some exercise. Just have your travelling companion watch your bags.

Depending on the season and sunset times, you may be able to visit the Cathedral of Palermo which dates from AD 1185. This is one of the gems of Italy. It is usually open till around 7 PM (19:00). It should be visited in the evening on arrival because you will want to spend more time the next day in Palermo shopping.

DAY 2- PALERMO & CATHEDRAL

Palermo is certainly worth at least a full day's visit. It is the capital of Sicily. There is much to see, you should consider extending your stay another day. The number one sight is the Palermo Cathedral built in the 12th century. This is a must visit because of its mix of architectural styles.

Consider taking in an opera in the evening at the *Teatro Massimo*. It is best to shop online for tickets, and do read the libretto so you know what's happening in the opera. In addition, the *Palazzo dei Normanni* is worth a visit. This palace with stunning Byzantine mosaics was built in the 9th Century.

There are four major street markets. The most popular is the *Bellaro* street market; in the port area you will find the *Vucciria* market. Do consider lunch at one of these market areas. There are many, many more sights to visit; just too much to mention. So it's best to obtain all online, or via a Sicily *only* guide book from Amazon.com

DAY 3- DAY TRIP TO AGRIGENTO

The Valley of the Temples in Agrigento is not to be missed. This temple complex is mind boggling. It is a place that should be on your bucket list. It is a UNESCO World Heritage Site comprising over 3200 acres. The temples were built about 600 BC by the Greeks to honor their gods. Here is a quick overview:

A main boulevard stretches about one quarter mile. Lining this boulevard are ancient temples built by the Greeks, then taken over by the Romans. There are about eight temples with many other fallen columns and other artifacts interspersed between them. Unlike the Parthenon in Athens and Stonehenge in England you can actually visit these remnants of antiquity. You can touch those ancient blocks of chiseled stone and sit on the fallen columns and ponder just how they were able to do all this without modern construction equipment. The site dates to the year 480 BC, about 500 years before the building of the Colosseum.

Of all the antiquity sites I have visited, this is absolutely the most impressive, second only to the Pyramids and Sphinx of Giza, Egypt.

It's quite easy to get to Agrigento by train from Palermo. Trains make the journey from Palermo Centrale to Agrigento *Centrale* on *Piazza Marconi* in two hours and the fare is only nine Euros each way. They depart every hour. On exiting the *stazione* in Agrigento (the last stop) you need to take a bus for one Euro to the Valley of the Temples which is about two miles away. You might also consider a taxi. Do ask before you get in the taxi what the fare will be.

You will need about two hours at the archeological site. There is lots of walking so it's preferable to go when the temperature is cool. The best time to arrive is noon and you should depart by 3 PM (15:00). I would strongly suggest that you try not to attempt a trip to Agrigento on a Saturday or a Sunday when the place is mobbed with people.

On departure from the archaeological site, you will find taxis waiting to take you to the *stazione* for your return to Palermo *Centrale*. For the day remember to take water and snacks with you. There are also several food carts at the entrance near the facilities. You should arrive back in Palermo no later than 7 PM to enjoy dinner.

DAY 4- BUS TO TRAPANI/ERICE

Just a quick word on why we go to Trapani/Erice for the next three nights. Trapani is a base we use to take day trips to the temple of Segesta (35 minutes) and on another day the temple at Selunite (one hour).

Trains leave for Trapani about every four hours and it's a 4-5 hour run. The journey by rail requires you to take at least one bus ride for a little over an hour and at least one train ride, most of the time two trains. By now you are thinking "are they kidding?" Remember my comment—I drove it with my rental car last year in 90 minutes! This is one of those cases *"where you can't get there from here".*

Now here's the best way to get to Trapani. Don't—repeat do not, take the train, take the *direct* bus! Several bus operators make the short run in about two hours. The cost is Euros and it is best to check with your hotel concierge on arrival in Palermo. These are blue buses, not the orange buses. In Sicily, blue buses are intercity buses and orange buses are within the city buses. The popular bus company between Palermo and Trapani is *Interbus* and their website is *interbus.it.* You can buy your tickets usually at the tobacco shops. Do check the departure points for the intercity buses and make sure you validate your ticket once you step on the bus.

Your bus will arrive at the main bus and train station in Trapani. By the way Trapani is pronounced "Trap-pan-nee." You have a choice to make. Where will you stay for the next three nights, Trapani or Erice (pronounced en-ree-chay)? So let me give you a quick overview of Trapani and Erice.

Trapani is a flat seaside port on the Mediterranean Sea. The main boulevard is the *Via Giovanni Battista Fardella* which is lined with restaurants, shops, high-end apartments, and condominiums. This wide boulevard ends at the city park, the *Villa Margherita,* (it's the only one). Buses and taxis can't continue since many of the main streets are pretty much pedestrian only. The main street here with all the shops is known as the *Corso Vittorio Emanuele.* This pedestrian way also contains the cathedral. However, when you get off the bus coming from Palermo, you will be only one block from the park. You can check into your hotel in Trapani located a few blocks from the train station or journey to the hilltop medieval town of Erice, which is my recommendation.

STAYING IN ERICE

If you are going to the hilltop medieval town of Erice, you can either take a taxi for about twenty Euros or take the funivia (cable way) *funiviaerice.it/*. This is not located at the train station but about two miles away. My suggestion, because of your luggage would be to take a taxi up the hill. You will have several other times to enjoy the funicular.

The *funivia* of Trapani-Erice, does not operate on windy days. Also, for most of January through March, it is closed for maintenance. The cost is about five Euros each way and I do not believe they take credit cards. However, if you do stay in Erice you will be able to take the cable car to Trapani and back on your day trips to Segesta and Selinunte, enjoying the breathtaking views of Trapani.

I might note that there are also buses which depart the train/bus station for Erice. However, figure about 25 minutes rather than the ten minutes by taxi, who I might note, will bring you directly to your hotel.

While there are many quaint hotels and B&Bs, my recommendation is to stay at the Hotel Moderno which can be booked directly at *hotelmodernoerice.it*. It's only a three block walk from the funicular when you set out for your day trips. I stayed here several nights and I can tell you, it's a gem. Do ask for a room with a balcony overlooking the street. Don't worry about those noisy crowds; they will be gone by 6 PM.

It is best to wander the streets of this medieval town and take in the flavor of it. Take a snooze, then go out to dinner at one of the many restaurants or just dine at the hotel and enjoy that great Sicilian food.

DAY 5- THE TEMPLE AT SEGESTA

The temple of Segesta predates the Greeks and Romans dating to 420 BC. It's so old they don't even know who built it. Historians believe it was the Elymians people. The temple itself is mesmerizing, sitting in a flat field. In addition to the temple, there is the ancient Greek theatre and many other Greek ruins.

So what I recommend is that after breakfast at your hotel you make your way back to the train station to catch the bus to Segesta. If you are staying in Erice, you will have to walk 3-4 blocks (from any hotel) to the funicular which will take you down to Trapani.

From the base of the funicular a taxi will take you to the main train/bus station for about ten Euros. It takes about ten minutes. Buses on a very frequent schedule also operate for about one Euro per person and take 20 minutes to arrive at the train/bus station.

Once at the train station you need to take a *Tarantola* bus to Segesta. *Tarantola* will take you to the entrance of the temple site in about 35 minutes. Plan on being there about two hours and do check the return schedule. The round trip costs about eight Euros. Most intercity buses have toilets on-board.

If you arrive early at the train station in Trapani to take your *Tarantola* bus to Segesta, it's best to pick-up a schedule and also ask the clerk, *"what time do the buses return from Segesta?"* Avoid taking the last bus for the day. If you cannot board the coach because it is full or it is canceled, you run the risk of a 200 Euro taxi back to Trapani or a lengthy taxi and train ride.

On arrival at Segesta, there is a café and souvenir shop and they do take credit cards. Clean toilets are available at the entrance before entry. There are also toilets and vending machines at the shuttle drop-off point for the Greek theatre. Seniors should not have to worry about doing all that up-hill walking.

Your admission includes a courtesy shuttle that will take you to the Greek theatre. Most people will take the shuttle; you need not be a senior. However, I believe you have to walk up to the temple itself which is in another direction from the main entrance. I might note that the shuttle to the Greek theatre allows you to take some exceptional photos of the temple off in the distance.

>>>TIP<<<
Try to get a seat on the right side (not the driver side) of the shuttle bus. This will afford you an unobstructed view for picture taking of the temple off in the distance.
>>>>><<<<<

DAY 6- THE TEMPLE AT SELINUNTE

Selinunte is another temple not to be missed. It is a Greek archaeological site and is located on the south-west coast of the island. It dates to about 600 BC. Only one temple of the five that were originally at this site remains standing. In its glory there were over 30,000 inhabitants of the city of Selinunte, which is actually in the village of Marinella. I won't bore you with all the details, but once again, unlike the Parthenon of

Athens, you can actually walk into this temple, view its construction and take loads of photos.

Selinunte, unlike the temples at Segesta and the Valley of the Temples in Agrigento, is actually on the coast. The remaining temple abuts the sea which makes a great backdrop for photos. You need about two hours here and do pack a picnic lunch. The reception center is new and there are clean facilities.

Now how do we get to Selinunte? There is one easy way to get down there and back, a train from Trapani to a town called *Castelvetrano.* It takes about one hour and fifteen minutes. However, there are not too many trains on this route. There is usually an early train about 8 AM. However, this will be a rush to get down to the station in Trapani by that hour. The second train is about noon, which will get you to *Castelvetrano* in a little over an hour. In addition once getting down to the *Castelvetrano* stazione you have to take a bus (*autoservizisalemi.it/*) for about 25 minutes. *Salemi* is the bus operator who will take your two Euros on the bus. Selinunte closes at 5 PM (17:00). So best is to avoid that last bus out and get the earlier one.

You might also consider skipping that great breakfast and getting that 8 AM train. Plan on leaving your hotel about 7 AM and get the *funivia* (funicular) or take a taxi from the main square in front of the *funivia* to the Trapani train/bus station (*stazione*). Once at the station, get your tickets to *Castelvetrano* and grab some nice pastries and a coffee to go.

>>>TIP<<<

Have your front desk manager print the train schedule to and from *Castelvetrano* the night before or better a few days before. Also, have him/her print the Salemi bus schedules from *Castelvetrano* to Selinunte.

>>>>><<<<<

>>>TIP<<<

If you happen to take the last bus back to the rail station at *Castelvetrano*, consider having dinner there about 6 PM (18:00). Several restaurants will be open at this hour. Consult *tripadvisor.com* for details. The trains back to Trapani depart at about 7:45 PM (19:45) with the last one at about 9 PM (21:00). Check before you depart Trapani in the morning.

>>>>><<<<<

DAY 7- TO PALERMO- FLY HOME

Once again this is one of those *"you can't get there from here"* situations. You take the same bus that brought you from Palermo. It's a two hour ride from the Trapani train/bus station to Palermo. If you are flying out of Palermo airport the same day, consider a bus the evening before and stay at a hotel in the lovely beach village of Mondello. You will need to take a taxi from Palermo *Centrale* to Mondello and a taxi the next morning to Palermo airport, about five miles away.

If you are not going to fly out of Palermo and instead continue your journey on the Sicily-East itinerary, it's better to take the first bus out to Palermo Centrale and then connect with the train that takes you to Taormina. Even the second bus is acceptable with a train connection that will get you into Taormina about 6 PM (18:00). Once you get to Palermo *Centrale*, trains depart about every hour for the other side (east) of the island. The run is four hours and costs 15 Euros. When the train gets to Messina *Centrale* make sure you are on the correct train bound for Syracuse and not Rome or Naples. If you fall asleep on the train you may find yourself on the Italian mainland and not heading toward Syracuse in the southeast corner of Sicily.

SICILY-EAST ROUGH OUT:

Day 1- Train to Taormina from Palermo, Rome or Naples (o/n Taormina)

Day 2- Taormina (o/n Taormina)

Day 3- Train around Mt. Etna, the Circumetnea Railway (o/n Taormina)

Day 4- Train to Syracuse (o/n Syracuse)

Day 5- Syracuse (o/n Syracuse)

Day 6- Train to Catania for your flight home or train back to Rome or Naples

DAY 1-ROME/NAPLES TO TAORMINA

If you are not arriving from Palermo after completing the Sicily-West itinerary, you will be arriving from Rome/Naples about 6 PM (18:00) or sooner. On arrival, check into your hotel. There are two choices here as there are two parts of Taormina. See my discussion under Day 2 below, on where to stay. You will have your choice of a hotel near the beach or atop the old city of Taormina

DAY 2- TAORMINA

People ask me all the time what's so special about Taormina? First, Taormina is an old city dating from 345 BC. It sits high on a hill overlooking the Straits of Messina. On any day you can see the Italian mainland. The town itself is steeped in history. There are lots of ruins in the center of the city, most of these dating to the Roman Empire. An interesting visit is the Roman amphitheatre which is of Greek design. It is known as the Ancient Theatre of Taormina.

Taormina is very much like the island of Capri today. About AD 1880 many of the rich and famous found Taormina a place to get away from the hustle and bustle of everyday life in the big cities. Writers and artists started flocking to Taormina. Gilt-edge, five star hotels were built for these rich and famous tourists and these hotels still exist today.

Many people do not know that there are two parts of Taormina. The Taormina everyone talks about sits high on a piece of solid rock almost 700 feet above the Mediterranean Sea, abutting the entrance to the Straits of Messina. This rock that comprises the city is by no means small. It is home to numerous hotels, B&Bs, restaurants, shops and, of course, gelato stands.

The other piece of Taormina sits at sea level and is a funky beach area, also containing numerous hotels, restaurants and shops. The Taormina everyone knows, high on the rock, is linked to the lower beach area by a funicular (*funivia*). The Taormina-Giardini *stazione* abuts the sea about one half mile south of the funivia in a small section of Taormina known as *Villgonia*. There are also numerous hotels in this area.

If you wish to stay in the city itself, best would be to take a taxi to your hotel on the rock. This will cost about 15 Euros. If you can afford it, and want to stay in one of those grand hotels where John Steinbeck and Truman Capote stayed, consider the Belmond Grand Hotel Timeo. On my last trip to Taormina, I slipped into the Timeo to have a cocktail and enjoy some olives and potato chips while watching the A-list people, not to mention the great views. And yes, I admit, I did use the facilities before walking down the path next to the hotel to the Greek theatre.

There is a certain feeling you get in Taormina. It's sort of like a magical town, a real "Disneyland" for adults. Shops and restaurants dot every street, however, they seem to be a higher class than you find elsewhere, as most of them don't sell all those goofy T-shirts and cheap souvenirs. Instead, you find shops selling products of Sicily, affordable works of art, gourmet regional foods and of course—gelato. The *Corso Umberto* a large pedestrian promenade with dramatic views of the sea at the far end offers over one quarter mile worth strolling. Expect to spend several hours here enjoying the local artists and the food carts. And most importantly, here is where you want to stay for a few nights. There are numerous classy B&Bs, apartments and hotels on the side streets connecting with the *Corso Umberto*. Enjoy Taormina; you will be here for two nights.

DAY 3- A TRAIN AROUND MOUNT ETNA

If you had a car you would drive around this dormant (for now) volcano. But, you could do it by train via the *Circumetnea* Railway. Note it is not Etna, but Etnea. It's a nice day trip and it's easy to do. You will have to consult the website *circumetnea.it/* to obtain the latest schedule. The railway now uses modern cars delivered in 2017 which have airline type toilets on board. The trains traverse farmland and lava fields stopping at several small towns over a five hour period. The route is an open circle around the volcano; like a big "C". Here's how it works:

Depending on the schedule, you take the Trenitalia train from *Taormina-Giardini* (it's the only station in Taormina) going south to Syracuse for about 15-30 minutes. You exit the train at *Giarre-Riposto* where you pick up the *Circumetnea*. From here the train chugs around Etna stopping at several towns before it reaches Borgo in Catania. From here you must take the Catania Metro (subway) to the main train station in Catania to get the train back to Taormina.

Depending on the schedule, you may have to originate your journey at Borgo and go counter-clockwise around the volcano to *Giarre-Riposto*. It may be difficult to exit the train at various towns since there may not be a train to continue your journey in the same direction. You should count on a whole day to circum-navigate Mount Etna. You should figure arriving back in Taormina about 7 PM (19:00) for that excellent Sicilian seafood dinner.

DAY 4- TRAIN TO SYRACUSE

It's less than a fast two hour run down the Ionian coast (part of the Mediterranean) to the ancient city of Syracuse. In Italian, it is known as Siracusa. The city is about 2700 years old and is the birthplace of Archimedes. The city has been inhabited by the Greeks, Romans and the Byzantine Empire. Trains depart *Taormina-Giardini stazione* about every hour and it's only about ten Euros. You can't get lost here as the *stazione* is the end of the line. What a deal!

What is nice about Siracusa is that it is a flat city and just delightful to stroll in. I love this city! It's divided into two sections. One is the western section where the train station is located and the other is the island of *Ortigia*. The island is separated from the western part of the city by a small canal about one hundred feet wide. You could swim it in five minutes but no need for this as there are two bridges.

The city contains two major areas of interest. On the mainland, is the western section, which is home to the Archaeological Park *Neapolis*. This contains the Greek amphitheatre constructed in 470 BC. In the same park you will also find the ancient Roman amphitheatre. Both theatres are in excellent condition.

On the island of *Ortigia* are the remains of the Temple of Apollo. It dates to about 570 BC and is the oldest Greek temple in Sicily. Also at the end of the island is the *Castel of Maniace*. The castle with its fortifications dates to AD 1232. You can walk the grounds for a small fee. There are numerous statues throughout the island. In addition there is a main square which is called the *Piazza del Duomo*. Lots of cafes and restaurants surround the square which is also home to the cathedral or duomo of Siracusa.

What I like best about *Ortigia* is the street market which is held every morning from 7 AM to about 1 PM (13:00), except Sunday. Here you can buy everything from olives and baked goods to fresh fish and products of the region. The market is plentiful with merchants selling all types of wine and olive oil.

Where should you stay when visiting Siracusa? I always recommend *Ortigia*. The cost of a room is not any different than the western side of the city. My favorite quaint hotel is the Hotel Posta. It can be booked directly at *hotelpostasiracusa.it/*. Do ask for a room overlooking the square and the canal. It offers an excellent breakfast and is within one block of the waterfront, the street market and that small canal which separates *Ortigia* from the mainland.

DAY 4- SYRACUSE

Siracusa is a walking town. After you explore the archeological park on the mainland on your first day here, consider taking it all in on *Ortigia*. After enjoying the street market, head over to the waterfront for the hour tour of the harbor for about ten Euros. Then have lunch at one of the many restaurants and cafes abutting the waterfront. Finish up your afternoon with a stroll through the *Piazza del Duomo* and some shopping, and yes—another gelato before returning to your hotel late in the afternoon for a siesta.

DAY 5- RETURN TO ROME/NAPLES OR FLY FROM CATANIA

You will need to either walk to the *stazione*, which will consume 30 minutes or take a taxi for about ten Euros.

Trains depart for Rome/Naples about 7 AM and 10 AM. However, if you are concluding your trip to Italy in Sicily, consider flying out of Catania (CTA) the other big airport in Sicily. You can fly from Catania to most European hubs i.e. Frankfort, Paris, Amsterdam as well as Rome and Milan.

The train schedule to Catania is very convenient as trains depart every hour or two. Intercity and fast regional trains make the run to Catania *Centrale* in a little over an hour for about ten Euros. You will have to take a bus or a taxi from Catania *Centrale* to CTA.

If you are back-tracking via rail to Rome or Naples, to start the Three Capitals Tour, Chapter 5, there are several through trains a day. If you do not get a through train you will have to change at Messina for the train bound for Rome and Naples. The journey is about 10-11 hours to Rome and 8-10 hours for Naples (Napoli).

Unless you are starting your rail tour in Sicily, this concludes the final itinerary of *ITALY—The Best Places to See by Rail, An Alternative to the Escorted Tour.* I hope you enjoyed your journey and that you will pass this information on to others who want to reap the benefits of a rail tour. I wish you well. Ciao!

My next chapter discusses the Florence day trips. I placed it at this point since these day trips create extra time needed to see Pisa and Lucca, Siena and San Gimignano and the Cinque Terre. All of these side trips add days to the Three Capitals Tour.

CHAPTER 10

THE FLORENCE DAY TRIPS

INTRODUCTION

If you have one or perhaps extra days, this is the place you want to enjoy them. Florence is a great base for day trips. Here I outline the four most popular: Pisa and Lucca, San Gimignano, Siena, and the Cinque Terre and how to get there by rail.

If you like natural mineral baths e.g. Saratoga, White Sulphur Springs, etc. then a day trip is in order to *Montecatini Termi*, only 50 minutes away. And, of course, if you are into wine, then less than an hour away you will find numerous vineyards in Chianti and the surrounding area, easily reachable by train from *Firenze*.

You can actually see all five sights i.e. Pisa, Lucca, San Gimignano, Siena and the Cinque Terre in three days if you plan your rail journey wisely. Pisa and Lucca will take one day and Siena and San Gimignano will occupy another. The Cinque Terre (the Five Towns), the seaside town of Manarola and perhaps another of the five towns will fill your third day.

So let's take a look at the five most popular from *Firenze* destinations and see how to get there by rail.

PISA AND LUCCA

Pisa and the medieval city of Lucca can be easily visited in one day. Trains depart about every hour from *Firenze's* Santa Maria Novella (SMN) station for Pisa. It costs about eight Euros one way. After finishing your visit to Pisa, it's only 30 minutes via direct train to Lucca. From Lucca you can take the train directly back to SMN, without going back to Pisa. This is all about an hour away from your hotel in Florence and it's simple to do. Here is how you do it:

THE LEANING TOWER OF PISA

Depart SMN no later than 10 AM for Pisa. You arrive about an hour later at Pisa *Centrale*. Do see if you can get an express train and remember to validate your tickets before getting on the train at those little yellow or green machines.

Once you arrive in Pisa you can hop a taxi, take the bus or walk the 20 minutes to the Leaning Tower complex. There will be plenty of people exiting the station en route for the Leaning Tower, so best to just follow the crowd and enjoy the 20 minute walk.

After visiting the leaning tower and the other buildings in the complex (the Baptistery, etc.) you need to find your way back to the Pisa *Centrale stazione* and head for Lucca. If you want to save your steps, summon a taxi or take a bus for about 15 minutes. I prefer the taxi since it's only 8-10 Euros. You will find taxis around the entrance to the Tower of Pisa complex at the taxi stands. If you are having a problem finding one, you can always walk to the closest hotel and they will summon a taxi for you if not parked out in front.

A few facts about the bell tower of Pisa. First, it was started in AD 1173, and completed about 200 years later. And, yes, it was 200 years later, not 20! It was not built to lean. It started slowly tilting because of the poor soil conditions below it. It tilts about 17 degrees. In the last thirty years engineers pumped concrete under its base to keep it from falling.

>>>TIP<<<

If you want to climb the Leaning Tower, you need to purchase tickets before leaving the USA. However, bear in mind that climbing the tower and waiting on line will consume almost two hours of your time and you may not be able to visit Lucca, unless you take a 9 AM train from *Firenze*. If you decide to climb the tower you can still visit Lucca, but it will be late in the day. You can always have pizza for dinner in Lucca or dine at one of the many *ristos* before taking an early evening train to *Firenze*. Trains operate every hour.

>>>>>><<<<<

The tower is 185 feet tall (about one third the height of the Washington Monument) and there are 297 steps to climb. If you are a senior, my suggestion is to seriously consider sitting this one out. If you have the energy, the ticket to climb those 297 steps costs a steep 18 Euros. And, get this, unlike the Statue of Liberty and the Washington Monument, there is no elevator. Repeat NO elevator. Also children under eight years of age cannot climb the tower alone, and must be accompanied by an adult and pay the full adult price. You will have to wait on line since your ticket is only a timed interval.

THE MEDIEVAL TOWN OF LUCCA

The train to Lucca only takes 30 minutes and costs about five Euros. Lucca is a medieval and Renaissance city which dates to the third century BC. It became an ancient Roman colony about 180 BC.

Lucca is a flat city and not on a hill like most medieval towns. There is no strenuous walking. It is a walled city with the train station just across the street from one of the city gates. Lucca is the birthplace of Giacomo Puccini the great opera composer, (*La bohème, Tosca, Madama Butterfly* and more). The streets are very enjoyable to walk with numerous shops, restaurants and cafes. This is an ideal place to enjoy lunch; which is far from the honky-tonk and commercialism of Pisa.

After enjoying Lucca, and of course, a gelato, you can catch the train back to *Firenze* SMN, (make sure you validate that ticket). This is not the same rail line you took to Pisa in the morning. So, if the stations don't sound familiar to you, don't worry. Just ask the train ticket-taker if the train is bound for *Firenze*. If he nods to you then you're on the right train.

SAN GIMIGNANO AND SIENA

You can visit two of the UNESCO World Heritage Sites and check off two more places from *"1,000 Places to See Before You Die"*. Of all the medieval towns in Italy, these are my two favorites. You can visit them both in one day since they are on the same rail line.

SAN GIMIGNANO DAY TRIP

San Gimignano, or San Gimi as it's known, is a hilltop medieval town about one hour southeast of Florence. It dates from ancient Roman times about 63 BC. It is a walled city with lots of shops and eateries. What is interesting about San Gimi is the towers. In the 14th century AD, families built these tall towers next to their homes to show their wealth. At its peak in history, there were 72 towers. Sadly, today there are only 13 still standing. Getting to San Gimi is not that difficult. As opposed to Siena, there is no actual rail station in San Gimi.

To visit San Gimignano, you need to take the train to *Poggibonsi* and then take a bus. If you take a direct train heading for Siena, you just get off at *Poggibonsi* and take a bus for about 25 minutes to San Gimi.

Trains to Siena depart every hour from Firenze SMN *stazione* and it costs only eight Euros to get off at *Poggibonsi-San Gimignano*. The train makes the run in about one hour. Buses to San Gimi from the *Poggibonsi stazione* leave every half hour. More info on the buses can be found at *tiemmespa.it*. By the way, the station before *Poggibonsi* is *Certalto* and is only 12 minutes away. So don't snooze on the train, else your San Gimignano day trip will be your Siena day trip in about 30 minutes after passing *Poggibonsi*!

The bus drops you at the San Gimi car park about three blocks from the main gates of the town. There are a few steps alongside of a modern supermarket and café before you reach a slight incline that will take you to the gates. From here it's a slight incline of walking on the *Via delle Romite*, which is lined with dozens of shops and restaurants en route to the main square, *Piazza della Cisterna*.

You will know you are in the center when you spot the cistern, known in English as the water well. On entering the *piazza* look to your right at about two o'clock and you will spot the old water well. If you have seen the movie *"Tea with Mussolini"*, it was filmed at the La Cisterna Hotel in the square. You may want to rent the movie again and then visit the hotel's lobby. There is lots of shopping in town mostly for products of Tuscany, some excellent places to have lunch, and yes, a gelato at the *Gelateria Dondoli*, which is billed as having the world's best gelato. You will find it right on the *piazza*. And yes, it is the best in the world! Take it from me, a true gelato aficionado.

SIENA DAY TRIP

Siena (sometimes spelled Sienna) is another hill top medieval town, built by the Etruscans about 900 BC. Like so many other sites in this book, it is also a UNESCO World Heritage Site and it's in "*1,000 Places to See Before you Die*". What is interesting about Siena is that the main square or *piazza* is not a square but a semi-circle. The *Piazza del Campo* is flanked by the *campanile* tower and the surrounding buildings are made of Siena red brick, hence where we get the color Burnt Siena. Sights to be visited include the Cathedral, the Basilica Cateriniana San Domenico, and of course the *Piazza del Campo* which is great for enjoying lunch on the square. Oh, by the way, if you enjoy pizza, this is the place for it. Shopping abounds in this town, so do bring a good strong day bag to collect goodies.

The Commune of Siena has made it easy to visit this medieval gem as there are escalators which take you from the *stazione* up the hill, so there is no need to walk it. Supposedly, the escalator in Siena is the longest in Italy. The escalator system will take you through several shopping malls before it brings you into the medieval city. You should figure at least 10-15 minutes on this moving stairway system.

Siena is quite easy to reach from *Firenze* SMN. Trains leave every 40 minutes and if you catch the fast train it will take 90 minutes. The cost is only nine Euros.

The train to Siena is the same train that stops at *Poggibonsi-San Gimignano*, which is the station you get off to visit San Gimignano. If you get a train out of Firenze at 9-10 AM you can also see both Siena and San Gimi in the same day. However, after doing all that walking in Siena you may not have enough energy to do more of it in San Gimi, especially if you are a senior. And remember, San Gimi is not like Siena—it's all up hill with no escalators. My suggestion is to visit San Gimi in the morning when you have your energy and it's nice and cool, then travel to Siena for lunch, sightseeing and shopping. Enjoy the day!

>>>TIP<<<

If you are going back to *Firenze* in the afternoon and stopping off at *Poggibonsi* to visit San Gimi, you need to make sure your train will stop there. Most of the regional trains (Regionals) will stop there. Ask the train conductor (on board ticket-taker) to make sure the train stops at *Poggibonsi*. And do make sure you validate those tickets in the yellow or green machines on the railway platform.

>>>>><<<<<

THE CINQUE TERRE DAY TRIP

You have probably seen pictures of this place and wondered where in Italy it is. Picture this, bright colored pastel buildings married to the mountain-side and washed by the sea. No, not Positano or Portofino, but the Cinque Terre, also known as the five lands. The five lands, from the south to the north are comprised of Riomaggiore, Manarola, Corniglia, Vernazza and Monterosso al Mare or just plain Monterosso. The coast line and the five towns are, of course, a UNESCO World Heritage Site and yes they are in the book by Patricia Schultz, "1,000 places to see before you die".

The five towns were inaccessible until about **AD 1900** when the Italian state government blasted tunnels through the mountains and laid the railroad tracks within a few feet of the Ligurian Sea, which is part of the Mediterranean. You have to visit the five towns by train since it is still extremely difficult to visit them by car or even bus. It is nearly impossible to visit all the towns in one day. Because of the time required to reach the Cinque Terre from *Firenze*, you will only have time to visit one town. My favorite and my recommendation is Manarola. So here is what you need to do:

From Florence, you must work your way to the town of La Spezia as there are no direct trains to the Cinque Terre. La Spezia is the rail gateway to the Cinque Terre from the South. Remember to pack some snacks and drinks for your rail journey. Most of the routings are via Pisa.

On arrival in *Firenze* check the train schedule for your fastest routing to La Spezia. Out of La Spezia *Centrale*, there is a train every 30-40 minutes to the five towns. Check the schedules. Some Regionals do not stop at every town, however, the Cinque Terre Express trains (so marked in the schedules) stop at all five towns.

You can also purchase a rail ticket which will allow you to visit as many towns as you can in one day for only twelve Euros. At most, on a day trip, you can really only visit two towns. Visiting three would be a stretch. So I do not recommend the Cinque Terre day Pass, since the fare between each town is only four Euros. When you purchase your tickets to the Cinque Terre, you need to purchase a ticket from Firenze to Manarola with a return. If you are returning from another town then specify that town to the clerk at SMN. You should purchase your local ticket from Manarola to one of the other towns locally.

Best is to depart *Firenze* SMN stazione first thing after breakfast about 10 AM. You can make the entire journey from *Firenze* SMN to Manarola with a train transfer at La Spezia in about two hours and forty minutes. By the way, don't worry about making your connection at La Spezia, the train will wait for you.

Just a note, after departing La Spezia it will be about seven minutes before the train stops in Riomaggiore. Don't panic if the station is all dark. Part of the station is in a tunnel. After departing Riomaggiore, collect your personal items and get ready to exit the train in three minutes at Manarola. Exit the train and follow the crowd through the walkway tunnel which is about the length of a football field. Bear to the left as you exit the tunnel and presto—you are in Manarola. The walk down the main street does not present a problem. There is a ramp which leads down from the small piazza as you exit the tunnel passage way.

Enjoy your lunch here whether it is a slice of pizza, a basket of fried calamari which you can stroll with or a sit down scrumptious sea food dinner. My favorite place is the Marina Piccola Restaurant at the end of the main walkway on the right. This place offers phenomenal views and good food at popular prices.

The rail day trip will cost 17-22 Euros depending on the time of day. You should plan on having lunch in Manarola and doing lots of shopping and catching a train back about 4 PM (16:00), which will get you back to *Firenze* SMN about 6:30 PM (18:30) just in time for a snooze and dinner at 8 PM (20:00).

>>>FUTURE TIP<<<

As of 2018 the *"Via Dell' Amore"* (the path of the Lover's) which links the towns of Riomaggiore and Manarola has been closed due to a landslide several years ago. This path which sits high on a cliff and hugs the Ligurian sea, allows tourists to walk the little more than a half mile between the two towns. The path is well paved and about 20 feet wide. Do not think of this as a dangerous gravel path! Once the path is reopened you will be able to enjoy the breathtaking walk. To walk the *Via dell' Amore* you will need to exit the train at Riomaggiore (half the station is in a tunnel) and follow the signs to the walk. You return via train from Manarola. There is a small fee imposed by the regional government.

Therefore when you purchase your tickets at *Firenze* SMN you must buy a ticket from *Firenze* SMN to Riomaggiore and a return ticket from Manarola to SMN. It is best to check the internet to see if the *Via dell' Amore* has reopened.

CHAPTER 11

SUGGESTED HOTELS NEAR THE STATIONS

INTRODUCTION

Some notes about hotels, reservations and other lodging suggestions:

Most of the hotels, including **B&Bs** and apartments, listed in this chapter, are close to the train stations. Either they are a short walk (less than 15 minutes) or a short taxi ride of less than ten Euros.

In the major cities there are hundreds of hotels within a short taxi ride from the station. Some of these hotels may be less expensive and a higher quality than my listings. You will note an asterisk (*) next to the listing if I stayed there and I am recommending it. As stated in the introduction to this book, I do not make any commissions or take any compensation for recommending these hotels or restaurants. In addition to the asterisk used to denote that I do recommend the hotel, I also indicate with a "W" if there is additional walking, particularly in the Venice Lagoon area. An "H" is short for Hotel (in the name of the lodging establishment) and BW means a Best Western hotel which is usually European in style.

If you do stay at one of the hotels I have recommended, please tell the front desk manager or the owner, that you found it in Bob Kaufman's book *"Italy—The Best Places to See by Rail"*. It may just earn you a free (gratis as they say) upgrade, grazie!

CHOICE OF HOTELS

When it comes to hotels, I can never figure people out. One couple I know of, checked into a five star hotel in Paris (I won't say which one) and checked out five minutes later because *"it wasn't their style."* In another example, I suggested a three star hotel about one block from the Spanish Steps in Rome. After reviewing it on the internet they felt it was too expensive to spend $200 a night to sleep. They wound up spending less than $60 at a two star hotel near *Termini* and were quite happy. Another thing I find hard to understand is why Americans enjoy staying at

American type hotels while in Europe. Why would you want to stay at one of those big American chain hotels (you know who they are) when you are in Europe? There is one exception, that being a stay at one of the airport hotels, where there are usually no European style hotels. So why not enjoy the ambiance of a European style hotel, or a B&B, and save those hotel points for use in the good old USA.

BOOKING ENGINES VS. BOOKING DIRECT

Feel free to use booking engines, such as *Orbitz.com*, *Booking.com*, *Hotels.com*, etc. for more selections. However, you may be able to get a better deal by looking up the actual or *official* website of the hotel you wish to book and then contacting them directly. Many times, they will give you a discount for a direct booking or if you are seniors, or if you are booking a longer stay than perhaps two days or if you are booking several rooms. Do email the hotel directly before making a reservation using one of the online booking engines. Sometimes you may not be able to cancel a reservation without a penalty using a booking engine. However, I have found that I can make a direct booking and cancel without any penalty if I give the hotel enough notice.

>>>TIP<<<

There is a lot of confusion or shall I say intentional misleading when it comes to locating hotels directly on the internet and making a direct booking (as opposed to using a booking engine). Let's say you want to make a booking at the "Moraye Hotel" in Sorrento. You located one of the first websites which states from your search page: "Moraye-Hotel-Sorrento-Reservations.com". You think you are booking directly. But you are not. If you check further down the search results pages you will find the "Official" website which is "Moraye-Sorrento-Hotel.it, which is owned by the hotel. It may even state "Official Website". This is the actual website you should use to make your reservation. The others are just "middle-men" collecting a commission of 10-20%. Truth is, they are probably not even in Sorrento or anywhere in Italy. They may not even know the hotel, Sorrento or even Italy. They only know what they can read off the official website. In summary, it is best to deal directly with the hotel.

>>>>><<<<<

>>>TIP<<<

If you are using the popular booking engines i.e. *Booking.com, Hotels.com,* etc., I suggest you don't pay the non-refundable price for a room which is usually less than the refundable price. Many times something comes up and itineraries change, so it's best to just pay a few Euros more with the satisfaction that you can cancel the reservation (per the policy) and get a full refund.

>>>>><<<<<

>>>TIP<<<

I suggest you check pricing on your hotels about two weeks before you start your trip. Many times prices drop and you will want to cancel and rebook with the lower price. This is another reason for not booking using a non-refundable price. You should also consider cancelling your booking a few days before you leave the USA if there is a non-refundable booking at a much lower price. However, make sure you are not into any penalty with the original booking. You should book the lower price non-refundable first and then cancel the original higher price booking.

>>>>><<<<<

I also use *hotelscombined.com* as a tool to finding hotels. Often hotels will only list on two or three booking engines i.e. orbitz.com, hotels.com, etc. If you are using *hotelscombined.com* you will usually get all the booking engines which the hotel has listed with. Have you ever heard of *hrs.com, amoma.com, otel.com* or *zenhotels.com*? There are hundreds of these booking engines. However, it's difficult and time consuming and nearly impossible to check out each booking engine. *Hotelscombined.com* does an excellent job at bringing all the listed sites together.

HOW TO READ HOTEL REVIEWS

I use *Tripadvisor.com* to review the quality of a hotel and decide if we should stay there. If you click on the reviews of the hotel, then add the **POOR** and **TERRIBLES** together, and if they exceed more than 25% of the total reviews, my suggestion would be not to stay there.

When reading reviews, you should discount the fact that the front desk manager was grumpy or the hotel had a rather small elevator. Look for more critical reviews e.g. "our sheets were dirty," or "we found dead bugs all over the place" or "we didn't feel safe leaving the hotel for dinner." Look for consistency in the reviews instead of isolated complaints. If you are happy with the praises, then make the booking.

GOVERNMENT RATING SYSTEMS

Unlike the USA where hotels are not government rated, the Italian government (and most other countries) rate hotels on a one to five star basis. In the USA the closest thing to this is the Automobile Association of America (AAA) which rates lodging establishments on a one to five diamond basis. Here are some points to consider when choosing a lodging establishment whether it be a hotel, B&B or alternate.

Generally speaking, did you know that for just a few dollars more, especially in Italy, you can usually stay in a four star hotel over a three star hotel? Some hotels you may stay in, which are government rated as four star ought to be a three star. Some three star hotels are priced over four star hotels. Over the years we have stayed in many three and four star hotels. We have found that the breakfasts at some of the three star hotels have been better than the four star hotels. No rhyme or reason, and frankly I do not understand the government rating system.

You should not think that a four star hotel will be better than a three star one, even though most of the time the four stars are superior in terms of amenities offered e.g. larger rooms, a lobby bar, room service, etc. Because I love those great Italian breakfasts, I look at the reviews about the breakfasts. If I see reviews about a four star hotel having just a so-so breakfast but a three star around the corner, having an out-of-sight breakfast, then I book the three star hotel even if it's a few Euros more.

When picking hotels you may also want to consider price and distance. It may be better to chose a four star hotel a mile away from the station for 100 Euros rather than a four star hotel for 180 Euros next to the rail station. Do ask the hotel a mile away what a taxi costs from the rail station to the hotel. So it may be a better deal to take the taxi.

Also, many hotels which are members of "chains" like Best Westerns and Accor allow you to book directly via their world-wide reservation services. Do consider direct booking with these chains as opposed to using the booking engines. They usually can provide you with discounts for AAA membership, senior status or multiple rooms. Their cancellation policies are usually more liberal than the booking engines. In addition, they can answer questions like "Can you have a room ready when we arrive from the USA first thing in the morning?" Or "can we have a quiet room facing the courtyard instead of the street?"

>>>TIP<<<

When checking into a hotel, you can always ask to see the room first. By doing this you won't have to lug your bags to another room when you find out the room they gave you was too noisy because it was on the street side. You can also ask the front desk "would you have any larger room, where you can provide us with a gratis upgrade?"

>>>>><<<<<

My list of hotels follows the itineraries described in this book. So the Roma hotels are listed first and Sicilian hotels last.

On a final point, with the exception of hotels I have made mention of in my chapters and where I have indicated in the hotel tables below with an asterisk (*), I do not recommend any of these hotels. I merely list them for your convenience. They are in no order. I have found over the years that it's best to read the reviews on *Tripadvisor.com* and make your own decisions. Also, remember, that you are only going to sleep there and have breakfast the next morning. You are not booking a room at a gorgeous beach resort, where you want to sip a pina colada while watching that beautiful sunset from your balcony!

Oh, and one point to remember again, which is strange in Italy, you must surrender your passport on arrival. When leaving the hotel for dinner or the day, give that one pound key back to the front desk clerk, they will appreciate it and so will your pocket.

Here are the hotels, most of them around the stations:

(YOU CAN MAKE NOTES BELOW)

ROME – TERMINI
All 4-Star

H Ariston	H Gioberti	Gioberti Art H
Una Hotel Roma	Bettoya H Med.	H Genova
Welcome Piram	Bettoja H Atlantico	H Aphrodite
BW H Royal	Smart H	Independent H

ROME AIRPORT (FIUMICINO) HOTELS
All 4-Star unless noted

Hilton Rome H	Hilton Garden Inn	Mecure Rome H
BW H Rome Apt	H Euro House-3	H Seccy
H Academy	H Tiber Fiumicino	Comfort H Roma
H Golden Tulip *	Sheraton Rome Apt	QC Terme Roma

FLORENCE –SANTA MARIA NOVELLA AREA
All 3-Star unless noted, except B&Bs

H La Scala	H Aurora	H Diplomat-4
H Ambasciatori-4	7 Florence B&B	Astrid H
Grand H Baglioni-4	H Universo	H Alba Palace
Rivoli Boutique H 4	H Croce Di Malta-4	H Boccaccio

VENICE-MESTRE STATION

H Plaza-4 *	BW H Bologna-4	H Tritone-4
Train Station B&B	H Regit-3	H Mondial-3
Venice Sweet Home	H Cortina	H Trieste

An Alternative to the Escorted Tour

VENICE-SANTA LUCIA STATION-THE LAGOON
W=not next to the station

H Spagna-3	La Locanda Di Orsaria-3	H Dolomiti-2
H Abbazia-3	H Universo Nord-3	H Belle Epoque-3
Arcadia Boutique-3	H Carlton Capri-3 W	H Ca Dei Dogi W
H San Moise W	Ca San Rocco W	Maurizio House W

MILANO CENTRALE

Colombia H-4 *	H Flora	Smart H Central
GLAM Milano-4	H Berna-4	Spice H Milano-3
Hilton Milan-4	H Bernina Milano	H Bolzano
H Michelangelo-4	Starhotel Anderson-4	Starhotel Echo-4
Canova	NYX Milan	Excelsior Gallia-5

TIRANO ITALY
All 3-Star unless noted otherwise

H Bernina	H Centrale-4	Albergo Meuble Stelviao
H Corona	Lifestyle Room Binario Zero	Albergo Gusmerol 2-Star

CHUR, SWITZERLAND

H Post Chur	H Drei Konige	Romantik H Stern
H Chur	ABC Swiss H	H Zunfthause zur Rebleuten

ZURICH HB, SWITZERLAND STATION
All 3-Star unless noted

H Limmablick	H Montana Zurich	Townhouse Boutique H
25 Hours H Langstrasse	H Arlette Beim Hauptbahnhof	Hotel duTheatre by Fassbind
H Bristol Zurich	Leoneck Swiss H	XTRA H
H Gregory-2	IQ130 Apartment H	H Alexander

ZURICH AIRPORT HOTELS

When you make reservations, do check if the hotel has complimentary shuttle service to and from the airport. If you are arriving on the train from Zurich, all you need do is go up to the arrivals area to spot your courtesy van to your hotel. Also, do email the hotel and find out if their shuttle van cruises the arrivals area or you have to call when you are ready to be picked up.

Movenpick-4	NH Zurich Apt-4	Holiday Inn Exp-3
Dorint-4	Raddison Blu-4	Ibis Budget-2
Park Inn-4	Hilton Zurich Apt-4	H Welcome Inn-3
H Fly Away-3	H Alegra-4	Swiss Star Apt

SORRENTO

H Antiche Mura-4*	H Plaza-4	H Tourist-3
Sorrento Flats	Tasso Suites	Casa Pantone
H Michelangelo-4	Grand H Cesare Augusta-4	La Ferrovia Guest House

PALERMO CENTRALE

Ambasciatori H-4	NH Palermo-4	H Porta Felice-4
H Palazzo Sitano-4	Locanda del Gagini-3	Art Lincoln Palermo-3
Palazzo Brunaccini-4	Grand H Piazza Borsa-4	Eurostars Centrale Palace-4
H Del Centrol-3	Al Decoro B&B	B&B Palermo Central

TRAPANI

Note- Hotel Moderno-2 below is a different hotel than the Hotel Moderno-3 of Erice.

Crystal H-4	H Vittoria-4	H San Michele-3
B&B Via Spali 52-	B&B Il Sole Blue	Albergo Maccotta-2
H Moderno-2	Residence la Gancia-4	Zibibbo Suites
Giardini Mon Plaisir-	Le Vie Di Trapani Apartments	Badia Nuova Residence

ERICE

H Moderno-3*	La Pinetaq Park H	H San Domenico-3
H Elimo-3	B&B Le Chiavi	H Edelweiss-2
Appartamenti Liberty-apartments	H Villa San Giovanni-2	Erice Pietre Antiche-condos

SIRACUSA-SYRACUSE
Best to stay on the island of Ortigia

H Posta-3*	UNA H One-4	Borgo Pantano-4
H Siracusa-4	Grand H Ortigia-4	H Grand Bretagna-3
H Livingston Siracusa-4	Algila' Ortigia Charme H-4	Grand H Minareto-5

TAORMINA

H Mediterranee-4	H Bel Soggiorno-3	Grand H Miramar-4
Amarita Apts	H Victoria-2	H Villa Eiorita-3
Villa Le Terrazze B&B	Mendolia Beach H-3	H Ariston and Palazzo-4

ALTERNATE LODGING

For security reasons, scams and logistics i.e. getting keys, etc. I am not a big fan of some of the newer websites which offer you a room or a couch to sleep on in someone's apartment. I have stayed at hostels and *pensione's* (in Italy), when Italy was $5-10 per day, and as they say, "been there, done that".

However, I do favor what is known today as a Vacation Rental. When we have to stay at a location more than four days, I usually shop the internet for an apartment. This gives us the ability to have a separate bedroom, bring in a take-away meal, sleep late without the maid banging on our door at **9 AM** and parking the car right outside our unit (when we are not taking the train, of course).

We use the typical search engines and select several apartments from a booking engine. Then instead of booking via the booking engine, I set out to deal directly with the owner. No middle person! I do not like to deal with a person thousands of miles from Italy, who has difficulty speaking English.

It costs me about the same as a three star hotel. I usually negotiate a small deposit which is taken by the owner via Paypal. I pay the balance on arrival with Euros. It's just like home and we get to meet the locals! Also, in Italy it is a custom to provide a welcome package of wine, crusty bread, eggs a quart of milk and an Italian salami. Very important!

CHAPTER 12

THE EURAIL PASS EXPLAINED

First of all, before going online and purchasing a Eurail pass from *Eurail.com* or *Raileurope.com* or your travel agent, it's best to read this chapter and do your homework first.

A HISTORY OF THE EURAIL PASS

To make visiting several European cities economical, as opposed to flying for example from Paris to Rome, in 1959 about a dozen European railroads i.e., Swiss Rail, SNCF (France), RENFE (Spain), DB(Germany) and FS (Italy) banded together to offer visitors from outside of Europe, an economical way to ride the trains rather than buying what is known as point-to-point tickets, which most of the time were more expensive. In addition, it was a competitive tool to be used against the growing airline business between the European city pairs.

Over the years several Eurail passes were offered and still exist today. Most popular are what I call the true Eurail pass and the other is the country specific pass.

Many first time visitors to Italy who would like to use this book and enjoy a stress-free rail tour think the best way to do this is with a Eurail pass. They obviously heard this from some friends at a back yard BBQ last summer. However, here are the real facts:

EURAIL ITALY PASS LIMITATIONS

First, there are two types of rail passes. One is the Eurail pass which is for travel between most of the countries (cities and towns) in Europe. The other is a country specific rail pass. The one for Italy is called the Eurail Italy Pass.

I won't discuss the Eurail pass, since we are not travelling from Rome to Paris. But here are the specifics for the Eurail Italy Pass.

First, the pass does NOT give you unlimited travel for the entire time you will be in Italy. Instead, it allows unlimited travel for so many days in a one month period. Rail passes are sold for unlimited travel for

3,4,5 and 8 days within the 30 day period. Here are more of the rules:

1. Passes can be purchased for first as well as second class travel throughout Italy, subject to other rules.

2. First class passes can be used in second class.

3. No type of Eurail or Eurail Italy pass can be used on the privately operated Italo trains.

4. The pass can be used on the Trenitalia network including all the high speed intercity trains and the Trenord trains in the north (Milan, Lombardy, and the Lakes District).

5. The Eurail Italy pass cannot be used on the *Bernina Express* since you would need a Eurail Pass or a Swiss Eurail Pass. The same holds true for travel from Milan to Lugano, Switzerland where you would need a Eurail Pass (not a Swiss Pass since part of the journey is in Italy).

6. Likewise, if you are continuing your travel to Zurich, you cannot use the Eurail Italy pass for travel on Swiss Rail from Chur to Zurich and further to the Zurich airport.

7.   Most reserved seat trains, i.e. the TGV (*Frecci-ETR*) style trains between Rome and Florence, require you to pay a reservation fee for the seat online or at the main train station, even though you have a rail pass. This ranges from three Euros to as much as ten Euros

8. If you are taking the Amalfi extension, you cannot use your rail pass on the *Circumvesuviana* Railway.

9. If you are visiting the Sicily-East area, you cannot use your Eurail Italy Pass, or any pass on the *Circumetnea* Railway around Mt. Etna.

10. On a positive note, many of the ferry companies which are state owned on Lake Como and Lake Maggiore do allow you to use all of the Eurail passes. However, these ferries are quite inexpensive, costing no more than ten Euros for a round trip ticket.

POINT-TO-POINT FARES

In the last ten years Trenitalia, Trenord, Italo and the RhB Railway (*Bernina Express*) have gravitated to the same fare pricing as the airlines. What I mean by this is that many point-to-point fares vary by time of day, whether they are refundable (or partially refundable)

248

or not, or purchased in advance, and discounted for seniors. Other factors also influence the rates i.e. connecting trains, direct trains, etc.

Some point-to-point fares discussed in this book vary from ten Euros for a morning train with non-refundable advance purchase to forty Euros with full refund for an evening train. In summary, I have found that the fares are all over the place.

The best approach is to add up all your fares on your planned itineraries. Then compare the total of all your point to point fares with a Eurail Italy Pass for the number of days you will be travelling within Italy. If I am correct, it will cost you more for the pass!

Also, remember that with the high speed intercity trains you will need to pay a reserved seat fee even with a rail pass either online or at the ticket counter.

Another way of looking at this is to take the cost of a second class rail pass for three days and divide it by three. The current rate for a three day Eurail Italy Pass is $207. This equates to $69 per day. If you take a look at all the itineraries discussed in this book, you will find that you can do most of them for well under $69 per day. That's strange you might argue, but true!

This cost analysis even gets worse with a Eurail pass as opposed to a Eurail Italy Pass. So save that three day Eurail pass when you want to go from Paris to Venice, then hop over to Amsterdam then to Athens!

And, let's face it, when you arrive at Rome airport and pay the say $20 fare on the *Leonardo Express* to whisk you to Rome's *Termini* station, you will not be in any condition to take another rail trip that day. Soooo— you either use your rail pass (that's one day gone) or you just pay the fare and put it on your credit card. Also, you should note that you cannot use your second class rail pass on the *Leonardo Express*. You must have a first class rail pass, since the entire train is first class only.

To reiterate you can't use your Eurail Italy Pass (and the regular Eurail pass) on the Italo trains which operate on the Rome-Florence, Florence-Venice, Naples-Florence, Venice-Milano and the Rome-Naples lines. What a bummer. In the writer's opinion, these trains are some of the best Europe has to offer and they are competitive with Trenitalia. Look at one of these sleek burgundy trains and you will want to take at least one rail journey on Italo.

In summary, unless you are travelling in one day from Milan to Palermo in Sicily, then taking the train a few days later to Venice from Palermo, you will not save any money by using a Eurail Italy Pass. In fact, it will probably cost you more. However, do check out the student fares and the family fares on all rail passes. Also, do not confuse the Eurail Italy Pass and the Eurail pass with passes offered by *Interrail.eu* which are strictly for European residents. If you want more information on the Eurail Italy and the regular Eurail pass, it is best to contact Raileurope (*raileurope.com*).

In summary—Eurail Italy Pass **NOT RECOMMEND**

CHAPTER 13

MONEY, CREDIT CARDS, TELEPHONES, INSURANCE, ELECTRICITY AND HOW TO PACK

MONEY

I have always found it far better to obtain my Euros out of an ATM in Italy, than going to my local bank in the USA. Also, as discussed in an earlier chapter, you should totally avoid going over to any of those money changers (*cambios*) at the airport or in Rome. They define the phrase "what is a rip-off."

Here is the best way to obtain Euros. I always suggest to my fellow travelers that after they arrive in their hotel in Rome, ask the front desk where is the closest ATM also known as a cash-point or a *Bancomat*. Let me explain why.

Once you get your bags and head over to the *Leonardo Express* station right at the airport, you will find that they take credit cards. So, no need for the cash. If your hotel is walking distance from the *Termini* stazione, you will not need any cash, except perhaps for a tip for the hotel bellman. If I don't have any Euros I will give any porter or bellman a few good old US dollars. They will certainly accept them. After my nap I set out to find a *Bancomat* with a suggestion usually from the front desk people.

You will be in for some surprises if you have not informed your bank that you will be in Italy for some time and will be using your bank card. So give them a call before you leave and set it up. Many banks allow you now to do this online. So just go back to your hotel room, take out your tablet or your smart-phone and set it up, or you can always call your bank. See below on how to call.

I find it's best to always get the maximum amount out of the machine. On most all non-Italian bank cards, the local bank in Italy only allows you to withdraw a maximum of 250 Euros per day from the *Bancomat*. The term "*Bancomat*" is a trade name of a consortium of banks in Italy. Many ATMs which are not *Bancomats* will still provide the same service.

253

Transaction fees vary by the US banks. Many US banks have reciprocal agreements with banks in Italy where the US bank waives the foreign transaction fee. I find it difficult most of the time to hunt down these specific ATM's to save a few dollars. However, expect to pay $12-$15 for your transaction. Therefore, it is senseless to just get 100 Euros out of the machine. Taking into account the current exchange rate in 2018 this equates to about a 10% fee assuming you only get 100 Euros. If you take out 250 Euros, your fee will be about 4% or less.

Don't get worried if you have too many Euros in your wallet at the end of your trip. You can always pay your last hotel bill partly in Euros and partly by credit card. You will find the *Bancomats* are very easy to use. Just press the ENGLISH button and you will get your instructions in English. As in the USA and elsewhere, best to visit your *Bancomat* during the day and not at night. Banks do have the Bancomats inside the lobby.

How many Euros do you need for a week? First, it's best to charge everything on your credit cards and only use cash for small items i.e. taxis (many now take credit cards), tips, souvenirs, street market items, and cafes. As a rule of thumb, I figure about 300 Euros a week for a couple. This is probably on the high side. It all depends how much shopping you do, how many times a day you swing into a café or a stand-up bar and have a café and a snack. Most of these places will prefer to take your Euros in lieu of a credit card which may make you look foolish.

There is no one Euro or two Euro paper notes. The smallest is the five Euro note. Coins indicated by a large "1" and a "2" are used for one Euro and two Euros. There are smaller coins which are the same as the USA i.e. cents, half Euros, etc.

>>>TIP<<<

It is best to keep the bulk of your Euros in a money belt and not in your pocket or your wallet. Italy is a very safe country, however, it is just being traveler savvy. So, after I get my Euros, I go back to my hotel room and stash them in my money belt or my money pouch that fits around my waist directly under my pants. This works especially for women since it is difficult to wear a money belt.

>>>>><<<<<

And one more point. Traveler's checks are usually not accepted anymore. If you can convince your hotel to take a few travelers checks, they will probably charge you an additional 5-10%. They served their purpose after WWII but now in the age of credit cards they are a thing of the past just like rotary dial phones.

CREDIT CARDS

Just like using ATM bank cards, you should inform your credit card companies that you will be in Italy for a certain time frame. Most establishments usually take VISA and Mastercard. Because of the higher merchant fees involved, many establishments will not take American Express. However, most hotels three star and above will. I find it best always to take two cards with me. You never know when that chip or magnetic strip will stop functioning.

Best to use a credit card where there are no foreign transactions fees. Many credit card companies convert the Euros on your transaction to the rock bottom bank exchange rate. However, they may add a 3% foreign transaction fee, for no reason whatsoever. So obtain a credit card(s) which does not carry any foreign transaction fees if possible.

If you don't have a credit card but have a bank debit card, you will find that all of the above transactions you can do with a credit card, you can also do with your debit card. Just make sure you have enough funds in your bank account before you leave home. Suggest you contact your bank before you leave to obtain another bank card just in case your chip or magnetic strip is worn. This will avoid a $100 overnight Fedex.

Also if you are interested in obtaining free airline points, hotel points or gift points, you ought to consider obtaining a points-based credit card. Just for obtaining the card, the issuer usually will give you 20,000-80,000 points for spending $1000 to $3000 on the card in the first 90 days. What a deal. It is best to check out the website *thepointguy.com* for an up to date analysis of the offers.

And there is one more point to consider: Many establishments, not just in Italy, but worldwide, will ask you sometimes on a Visa, Mastercard or other charge card transaction, if you would like to pay in Euros or US dollars. The answer is to always pay in Euros. When you offer to pay in dollars they will be giving you their exchange rate which is usually not the rock bottom exchange rate you will receive from your bank once the transaction is posted and converted from Euros to Dollars on the day of the transaction.

TELEPHONES AND CALLING

Because of new technologies developed in the past five years, there are now many ways to make telephone calls back to the USA and even local calls. Let me go over most of these alternatives.

>>>TIP<<<

With the exception of a local call or an 800 call, try not to make any calls from your hotel room and charge it to your room bill. You will find that the rates charged will be astronomical when calling back to the USA or in fact other points in Italy. It is best to check first with the front desk before any surprises about a ten minute call back to the USA for a whopping $79.

>>>>><<<<<

TELEPHONE TRAVEL PLANS

Many national cell phone providers i.e. AT&T, SPRINT, Metro PCS, T-Mobile and Verizon offer foreign travel plans for travelling abroad. They usually give you a package plan but after those usually **100** minutes per month expire, they charge you about

$2.00 per minute to call the USA and also to receive calls from the USA.

The travel plans also offer a small about of data and text messages. For example, Verizon offers 250 Megabytes per month and 100 text messages on its monthly travel plan in addition to 100 minutes of in/out calling. As of this writing, the Verizon plan discussed is about $40/month per phone. Other plans are available. The allowance of 250 Megabytes does not go far. You will certainly use this up very quickly if you are transmitting pictures of your vacation or viewing your Facebook account without the use of WIFI or any other form of direct internet access. If you are not using WIFI from your hotel room and are using the cell phone system, expect a jumbo cell phone bill when you get back to the USA. Contact your cell service provider for more information and do discuss a travel plan so you can use your cell phone.

ITALIAN CELL PHONE

For as little as 40 Euros, you can purchase an Italian cell phone with a SIM chip in it. This is called an unlocked phone. The SIM card placed in it determines your carrier and your phone number. You can recharge the phone at numerous locations, including those ATM *Bancomats* described above. Two of the largest providers are Vodafone and TIM. Rates are much less expensive for calling back to the USA. Best to visit a cellular store (there is one at *Termini Stazione*) and check the rates before you purchase it. Also, the phone comes in handy when you have to call a restaurant or your hotel. They are quite simple to use with just a few Italian words which you can figure out in a few minutes. Your front desk clerk will be able to locate a nearby shop. Do enquire about the open and close times since many are closed for the siesta period.

TELEPHONE CARDS

This is an easy one. You purchase a ten Euro phone card at your local tobacco shop or anywhere they are sold. You then dial an 800 number (toll free from any phone), you key in your card number, and then the phone number you wish, and presto, the call is made. This costs far less than the travel plans offered by the US cell phone service providers. It is not necessary to deposit any coins (or a phone card) in a pay phone to dial an 800 number. However, it is best to keep a Euro in your pocket if needed. It will be returned after you dial the 800 number. Also, bear in mind that sometimes hotels do charge to make an 800 call which defeats the purpose of using a telephone calling card. Best to use a public coin (or card) telephone.

You should also note that telephone numbers in Italy are different or should I say "odd". They use multi-digit phone numbers. For example a hotel in Rome may have a five digit number like 89300. However, if you call the restaurant next door, they will have a nine digit number 874 989 876. If you need help you can always ask someone to help you dial the number. It's not a big deal (prego).

GOOGLE PHONE/ SKYPE/ FACETIME AND FACEBOOK MESSENGER

New internet technologies have emerged in the last five years which allow us to use WIFI internet access to bypass the local telephone companies most of the time.

GOOGLE PHONE

There is no charge for obtaining a Google phone number, sometimes called Google Voice. It's a regular American telephone number complete with area code. You will need to originate the call only when you are connected to the internet, usually via WIFI. If you are calling another person who is also connected to the internet, the call will go through with no problem over the internet and bypass the public switched telephone network (PSTN) completely. However, if you are going "off-net" i.e. the other phone is not connected to the internet i.e. it's a landline or a cell phone you will have to pay a small connection charge for the call. This amounts to about 2-3 cents a minute. This is because Google has to "dump" the call into the public telephone network and pay a local telephone company e.g. Verizon or Century Link to complete the call. So, in order to do any off-net calling on a Google number, you will need to charge your account for at least $10 or $20 for an allotment of minutes. The funds don't expire and you can even use them in the USA to call a hotel in Italy. You must also download the Google Voice App to your smart-phone, tablet or PC. And yes, to re-iterate, you must have WIFI or direct internet access to originate the call.

I might note, you can also call into your Google phone number. However, if you have a 212 area code and your friend calls you from area code 609 there may be a charge for the long-distance call from the originating telephone company.

In summary, what I usually do while in Italy is use my Google number first; if that has a problem (usually because of insufficient bandwidth) I make the call on my Italian cell phone or my American cell phone.

FACETIME

Skype and FaceTime (FaceTime is a trademark of Apple Inc.) also can be used, but unlike the Google number they only can provide WIFI or internet calling to internet calling. Either the originating iPhone or Apple tablet must be connected to the internet and the receiving device. You can't go off-net to a landline. FaceTime only operates on "Apple" devices. Apple is a trademark of Apple Inc.

SKYPE

Skype can also be used on iPhone as well as non iPhone devices. You need to download the app and have the proper operating system. Skype is a trademark of Skype Technologies SARL. Unlike FaceTime, Skype allows you to go off net just like Google Voice. However, like Google Voice you will need to charge your account.

FACEBOOK MESSENGER

You also may want to consider using "Facebook Messenger" which is a trademark of Facebook. You can do texting via the internet as well as video chats. Once again, you need WIFI or a direct internet connection. If you text a lot, this will not eat up your texting allotment on you cellular travel plan.

BANDWIDTH RESTRICTIONS

Be aware that many larger hotels restrict high bandwidth applications from hogging their pipeline to the internet. Running FaceTime or Skype may slow down other applications being run by other guests e.g. checking their emails, etc., so you will not be able to connect via some of these newer WIFI/internet technologies. If you do connect, often you will be allowed two or five minutes of connect time. So get prepared for the local WIFI system to drop you out after the set time duration.

ELECTRICITY REQUIREMENTS

Europe has a different voltage system than North America. The system used in Italy is 220 and not 120 volts. You don't have to bring a special 220 volt hairdryer. Most hotels do have hairdryers in the rooms. If you don't find them in the room, just ask the front desk. Ladies, if you use a curling iron; best to pick up a 220 volt unit in Italy. If you are bringing any other device which operates on 110 volts, you need to bring a one pound 220 to 110 volt converter (transformer) and obtain a physical converter plug for operation in continental Europe, (this may also come with the transformer).

If you are going to be charging your cellular phone, tablet or PC, you can either purchase a one pound 220 to 120 volt converter to lug around or better just get yourself a 220 volt USB charger. They are inexpensive and you can purchase them on Amazon. The chargers all have a USB output, so just plug in your cord. At my first street market I usually pickup a few spares for less than four Euros each, since these items burn out often and you don't want to go racing around to find a replacement. Also, most of the newer high speed intercity trains i.e. the *Frecci's* will have USB chargers built into the seats or side panels.

MEDICAL INSURANCE

Seniors who have their medical insurance with Medicare are NOT covered while out of the country. If you have a supplement they usually will not pay anything unless Medicare pays first. This will not happen in Italy and outside the USA. So you need some type of medical insurance.

It is best to check online or with your present insurance carrier if not Medicare. Make sure the insurance coverage includes accident and sickness.

Some of these travel insurance providers to name a few are *insuremytrip.com, allianztravelinsurance.com,* and *travelguard.com.*

You can also purchase a yearly policy that will cover you if you are a frequent out of the country traveler. Make sure they will also cover your travelling partner. Many of these policies also contain trip cancellation and trip interruption provisions if you need to come home early for some "covered" reason. If you have to use the policy abroad, always check first with the insurance company and do have your policy with you.

Also remember that Italy is a first class modern country and they will provide you with medical and dental attention equal to or better than what you would expect to receive in the USA.

HOW TO PACK

You must pack a little differently for a rail trip than you would for an escorted tour. First I recommend a piece of luggage that is lightweight and has wheels. The piece of luggage should not weigh a lot. It should be no more than 24 inches in length and no more than 14 inches in height and width. If it has one of those pull out handles, more the better. And do consider the new bags which have lots of outside zipper pockets.

Now, what do you pack? First, you will need a comfortable pair of walking shoes or sneakers. Do not try to "break-in" a pair of shoes or sneakers on a trip—bad idea. Ladies, do not bring an extra pair of shoes and do leave those high heels home. Save them for the cruise. I usually suggest only one pair of shoes, the ones you wear. Every time I take a dressy pair of shoes to wear to a nice place for dinner, I find that everyone else is wearing sneakers.

Italy is a laid-back place, however they will get dressed up for a nice Sunday afternoon dinner. So guys, you will have to take the T-shirt off and put on something more "dressy-casual".

The whole concept in packing is to pack light. We use lots of large one gallon zip lock bags so we can see everything we pack. If you are going to be on your trip for more than 12 days consider that you may have to spend a few hours in a laundromat (*lavanderia a gettoni*) with the locals. It's not a big deal and you may even learn some Italian.

If you are renting an apartment in Milan when you are visiting the city and the Lakes District, make sure your unit has a washing machine. Men should lighten the load by taking khakis instead of heavy jeans. Consider only one sweater and a light jacket. Bring those travel sizes of shaving cream, etc. Put only the number of meds you need plus a few more in a plastic sandwich bag instead of taking that heavy bottle. And forget the bathing suits and the tennis rackets!

Now, after you are fully packed, remember this—you will only wear about 50-70% of the items in your bag. So un-pack it all and say to yourself "what can I do without"? Also, remember that you can always buy that nice shirt in the Saturday street market in Rome, Milan or Palermo or any city or town I have mentioned in this book. You need to also allow space to bring home all those souvenirs you buy. Make sure you have no more than 30-35 pounds in each bag, since the limit is 50 pounds (23kg).

It is best to take only one carry-on bag for two people. Sometimes you can avoid this completely and just stay with your two pieces of luggage (per couple) and pack any carry on items in a lightweight carry bag which you pack in one of those two big bags. It's just easier for rail travel. Do pack your medications in your carry-on bag. We also pack a lightweight "day" bag. I carry it on my shoulder with my books and maps, and of course, my tickets and other travel documents. And do carry your passports on your person and not in any bag that can go astray.

I think that wraps it all up.

IN SUMMARY

I do hope you enjoyed this book. As stated in the introduction, it is not an entire travel guide to seeing all of Italy via train. It is intended to provide a day by day itinerary for seniors, and in fact everyone, to visit the highlights of Italy without having to spend an awful lot of money on an escorted tour.

So do enjoy this beautiful country and reap the benefits of rail travel! Ciao for now and hopefully we will see you in Italy.

BLANK PAGE FOR NOTES

APPENDIX

An Alternative to the Escorted Tour

SUMMARY OF TRAIN INFORMATION

CONTINUED ON NEXT PAGE

CITY-PAIRS	TIME	FRQ	EURO
ROME FCO - ROME TERMINI	30m	2/hr	14 (1)
ROME-FLORENCE	1h/30m	2/hr	20-25
FLORENCE-VENICE	2h/5m	1/hr	25-30
VENICE-MILAN	2h/13m	1/hr	20
MILAN-STRESA	56m	1/hr	10
MILAN-VARENNA/ESINO	1h	EOH	7
MILAN-LUGANO	1hr/15m	EOH	24
MILAN-TIRANO	2hr/32	EOH	12
TIRANO-CHUR	4h	1/dy	Varies
CHUR-ZURICH	1h/15m	1/hr	20
ZURICH-ZHR AIRPORT	12m	6/hr	4
ROME-NAPLES	1hr/30m	2/hr	15-20
ROME-PALERMO	11hr	5/dy	50-90
ROME-TAORMINA	9hr	5/dy	33-75
NAPLES-PALERMO	9hr/20m	4/dy	30
NAPLES-TAORMINA	7h	7/dy	26-65

SUMMARY OF TRAIN INFORMATION CONTINUED

PALERMO-AGRIGENTO	**2h/4m**	**1/hr**	**9**
PALERMO-TAORMINA	**4hr**	**1/hr**	**15-30**
TAORMINA-CATANIA APT	**1hr**	**2/hr**	**5**
FLORENCE-PISA	**1hr/10m**	**3/hr**	**9**
PISA-LUCCA	**30m**	**2/hr**	**4**
LUCCA-FLORENCE	**1h/20m**	**2/hr**	**8**
FLORENCE-LA SPEZIA	**2h/20m**	**1/hr**	**14**
LA SPEZIA-MANAROLA	**10m**	**2/hr**	**4**

Notes:
(1)- all first class, if using Eurail pass it must be a first class Eurail pass

TABLE OF POPULAR
OFFICIAL WEBSITES

RESOURCE	WEBSITE
Trenitalia	Trenitalia.com
Trenord	Trenord.it
Italo	Italotreno.it/en
Colosseum of Rome	Coopculture.it/en/colosseo-e-shop.cfm
Roman Forum	Same as above
Vatican Museum	museivaticani.va/
The Academy	Accademia.org
Uffizi Gallery	Uffizi.it/en
Tower of Pisa	Towerofpisa.org
Waterbuses Venice	Actv.avmspa.it
Ferries Maggiore	Navigazionelahi.it
Ferries Como	Same as above
Lake Lugano Info	Lakelugano.ch/en
Bernina Express	rhb.ch
Swiss Rail	Sbb.ch/en/home
Rail bookings	Raileurope.com
Metro Rome	Atac/roma.it/

Metro Milan	*Atm.it/en*
Circumvesuviana	*Sitabus.it*
Circumetnea	*Circumetnea.it*
Metro Palermo	*Cittametropolitana.pa.it*

Notes:

1. Book Intercity reserved seat trains as soon as possible. Many popular routes and times of day sell out fast. In addition, seats that are deeply discounted, like the airlines, also sell out fast.

2. For Trenitalia, Trenord and Italo, you can only book a train within the 120 day departure window.

3. On the websites, many times you MUST use the Italian name for the city e.g. use *Firenze*, not Florence, else it will show "no such station".

3. There is no need to make a reservation for trains which are not seat-reserved.

4. Best to deal directly with the museum or attraction's "official" website when purchasing tickets. Many independent ticket agencies mark-up or add a fee to the ticket prices.

5. If you have purchased your tickets before your trip, make sure you go to the head of the line and ask

where to line up if you have your tickets already. Most attractions have two lines, one for the ticket holders and one to purchase tickets.

6. Suggest you pack your internet and your rail tickets, etc., in your carry- on bag with copies in your main luggage bag. If your bags go astray you will still be able to enjoy Rome for a few hours or days before your bags are delivered to your hotel.

7. *Bernina Express,* on main website is German, just change the "DE" to "EN" for English. Also there is a 90 day booking window. If travelling in July or August book on-line immediately, else you will need to spend an extra day in Tirano or Milan if the day of travel on the *Bernina Express* is sold out.

STATIONS/TOWNS MENTIONED

Rome Airport	Milano Centrale	Pompeii
Rome Termini	Varenna-Esino	Isle of Capri
Florence SMN	Bellagio	Palermo
Pisa Centrale	Como	Trapani
Lucca Centrale	Stresa	Erice
La Spezia C.	Baveno	Agrigento
Montecatini	Lugano	Castelvetrano
Poggibonsi (1)	Tirano	Selinunte
Siena	Chur (CH)	Segesta
Riomaggiore	Zurich HB (CH)	Messina C.
Manarola	Zurich Airport	Taormina
Corniglia	Naples	Catania
Vernazza	Sorrento	Borgo-Catania
Monterosso	Positano	Giarre-Riposto
Padua	Amalfi	Siracusa

Venice Mestre	Ravello	Ercolano
Venice SL	Praiano	Certalto

SMN- Santa Maria Novella
SL- Santa Lucia
C.= *Centrale*
(1) – Station name is *Poggibonsi & San Gimignano*
CH= Switzerland

ROME-FIRENZE-VENICE
TIGHT-9DAYS
COMFORTABLE-12 DAYS
RELAXED 14 DAYS

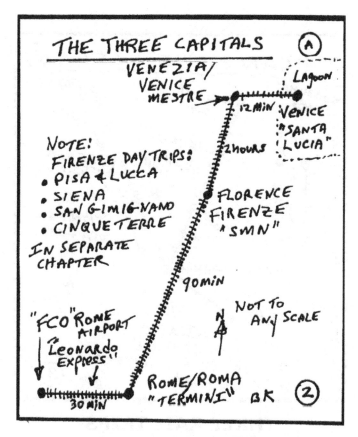

THREE RAIL TRIPS
BEAUTIFUL COUNTRYSIDE
ALL TGV STYLE TRAINS

An Alternative to the Escorted Tour

MILAN AND THE LAKES
TIGHT- 4 DAYS
COMFORTABLE- 6 DAYS
RELAXED – 8 DAYS

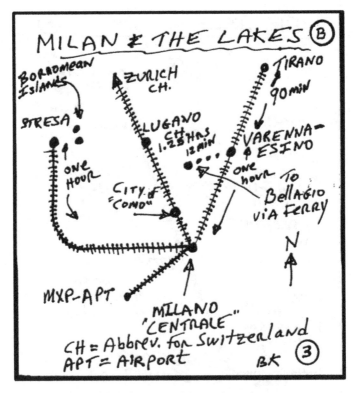

THREE RAIL TRIPS
BEAUTIFUL TOWNS/LAKES
MILAN-SIGHTS

280

THE BERNINA EXPRESS
TIGHT- 3 DAYS
COMFORTABLE- 4 DAYS
RELAXED – 5 DAYS

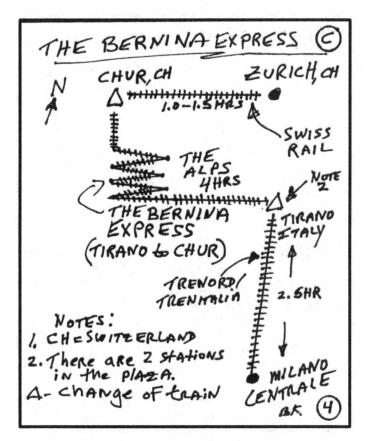

THREE RAIL TRIPS
SPECTACULAR SCENERY
A UNIQUE RAIL TRIP

An Alternative to the Escorted Tour

AMALFI-NAPLES-SORRENTINE-CAPRI
TIGHT-5 DAYS
COMFORTABLE-6 DAYS
RELAXED 7 DAYS

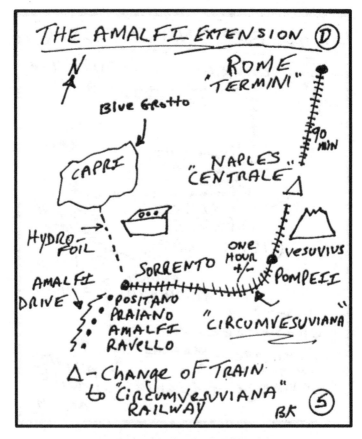

TWO RAIL TRIPS
AMALFI DRIVE & POMPEII
ISLE OF CAPRI

PALERMO-TRAPANI-ERICE
TIGHT-6 DAYS
COMFORTABLE-7 DAYS
RELAXED 8 DAYS

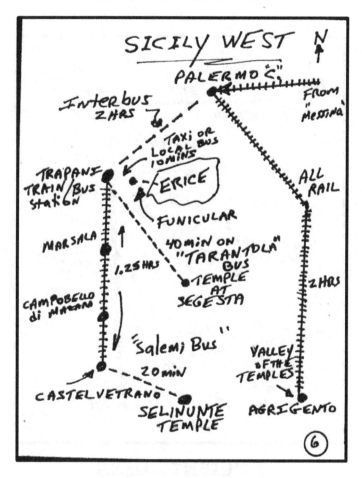

THREE RAIL TRIPS
ANCIENT TEMPLES
MEDIEVAL ERICE

TAORMINA-SYRACUSE-MT. ETNA
TIGHT-4 DAYS
COMFORTABLE-5 DAYS
RELAXED-6 DAYS

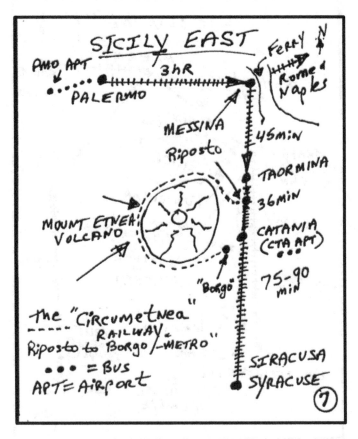

ANCIENT RUINS
LOTS OF SHOPPING

PISA AND MEDIEVAL LUCCA
TIGHT- ONE DAY
COMFORTABLE- ONE DAY
RELAXED- ONE DAY

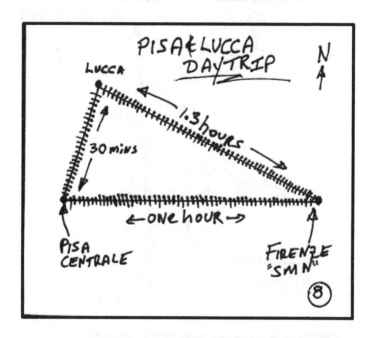

THREE RAIL TRIPS
LEANING TOWER OF PISA
BOTH CAN BE DONE
EASILY IN ONE DAY

ONE COMFORTABLE DAY TRIP
TWO MEDIEVAL TOWNS
THREE RAIL TRIPS

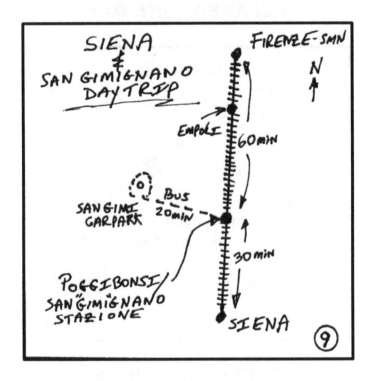

THE FIVE TOWNS ON THE LIGURIAN SEA
TIGHT- ONE DAY
COMFORTABLE- TWO DAYS
RELAXED- THREE DAYS

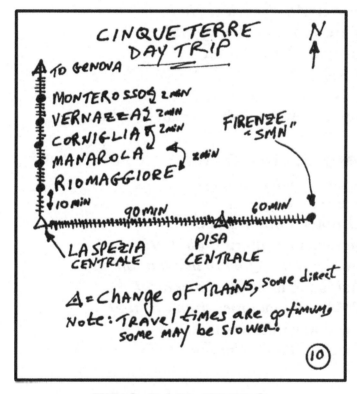

TWO RAIL TRIPS
BEAUTIFUL SCENERY
INTERESTING PLACE TO VISIT

TRAVEL PHASES MADE EASY

Basics:
Please: *Pour Fah Vor Ray*
Thank you: *Grat zee*
Hello: *Bon jor no*
Goodbye: *Ah river dear chee*
How are you: *Comb may stah*
Excuse me: *Me skoo zee*
Yes: See
No: No
Do you speak English: *Par lah Engleze*

Where is: *Dough - vay*
Station: *Sta zee onay*
Toilette: Bag no
The hotel : *hotel xxxxx*
The ticket counter: *biglietteria*
How far is it?: *Quanto aye lan ton oh*
What is the fare: *Qual a la tariff*
ATM bank machine: *Bank co mat*
How many minutes to xxxx:
   Use *Quanti minuti a* xxxx

Eating:
I would like a menu: *Vo ray eel me new*
I would like the check: *Me porta eel conto*
Take credit cards: *La carta dee credito*

An alternative to the four hour bus tour is to see the highlights of monumental, ancient and Catholic Rome on one of those hop-on-hop-off buses. These buses provide an overall orientation with a narration tour, but do not include any visits to the sights. You can go back and visit these sights later in the day or in the evening. If you do get off to visit sights on the route, you must also consider the wait time for the hop-on-hop-off double-decker bus to return, so you can hop-on and continue. Also, there is time in the afternoon after visiting the Vatican and on Day 4 to do this type of touring as a wrap up of anything that you haven't seen already.

>>>TIP<<<

When reviewing the websites or brochures from these day or half day tour operators, it's best to pay close attention to the word "visit." If it does not say "visit" next to the Colosseum, the bus will only do a drive-by.

>>>>><<<<<

If money is not a determining factor, consider booking several of these four hour tours instead of doing it yourself i.e. taking a taxi to the Vatican, etc. My suggestion would be to book the tour which includes the Vatican Museum and St. Peter's Basilica.

Tickets are provided and you won't have to stand in a half mile long line to gain entrance to the Vatican Museum. Most tour guides on these city tours are state, city or Vatican certified and really know their stuff. Make sure you book an English speaking tour or make sure there are headsets on the bus in several languages. You will find most of this information in the hotel brochure or on the official websites of the day tour operators.

Private tour guides are available. However, unless you have a group of 4-8 this tends to be very pricey. Certified tour guides, which are mostly union (called guilds) run 50-80 Euros per hour with a minimum of four hours. In addition, visiting the Vatican Museum requires an additional certification. In other words, if you hire a guide for the day, that guide may not have certification to take you through the Vatican Museum and narrate all those details. However, they will be able to take you through St. Peter's Basilica.

If you are looking for a private guide to take you and perhaps another couple or two around Rome for the day, best to consult the internet. You will find them usually by searching for "Tour guides in Rome Italy". Do make sure they have City of Rome certification. Some may even have Vatican Museum certification.